BEGINNER'S DOG GUIDE

Your Dog's First Year

Dr Rachele.M.Lowe

B.V.Sc (hons)

NEW
HOLLAND

Acknowledgements

This book was made possible with the help of so many family, friends and colleagues.

A special thank you to my husband, Siôn, who upped his share of household duties while I was writing, and provided me with endless cups of tea!

Thank you to my parents, Michele and Peter. You are a wonderful source of encouragement and your pride in me is an inspiration.

Sophia, Celeste and Matt—your encouragement and faith in me was also much appreciated.

Thanks must also go to my business partner, Chris, who was endlessly patient with me during my absences needed for researching this book.

Thanks also to the wonderful staff at Mosman Vet Hospital for their enthusiasm.

Thanks to my manager, Matt Clarke from MCM and New Holland Publishers, without whom this opportunity might never have happened.

A special thank you to my wonderful clients and patients—they are what makes being a vet the best job in the world.

For my extraordinary canine companion,
Minou,
and my darling sons
Callum and Shannon—the best boys in the world.

Contents

3: The medical stuff 32

4: Manners maketh the pet 68

1
So you think you want a dog

Dog ownership has long been part of our modern lifestyle. It is no surprise that dog ownership is on the increase. Dogs offer a welcome relief from the hustle and bustle and stresses of modern life, and the increased loneliness and anonymity that comes from longer working hours and little down time. No matter how your day has been, Fido will always be waiting, tail wagging, eyes alight with joy at your homecoming. You are his hero.

Pet ownership has been found to have measurable benefits to our health. As well as saving us from loneliness, several studies have revealed that people who own pets typically visit the doctor less and use less medication, have lower cholesterol and triglyceride levels, recover more quickly from illness and surgery and deal better with stressful situations.

My experience with my own dog, Minou, has been a testament to the joys life with a canine friend can bring. When Minou came into our lives, I had no real intention of getting a pet. My husband and I had just returned from a year overseas and were busy settling into new jobs, and a new, quite small, city townhouse. We already had a feline child substitute, and I was quite happy doting on my canine patients in place of a dog of my own.

My husband, Siôn, had other ideas. He and a friend organised a lunch trip to the other side of the city with the secret mission of visiting another friend whose dog had puppies. There was little Minou, the last puppy left with no home, staring up at us with loving big brown eyes. Without a second thought, Siôn scooped the little Poodle cross pup up into his arms and refused to let her go.

From that day on, Minou has been our constant companion. Siôn, who was initially sceptical about taking a poodle on walks in public (as a child, he only ever had big dogs, usually German Shepherds) was delighted to find fluffy little white dogs were great conversation starters and 'chick' magnets. Having a dog changed the focus of our lives immediately. Instead of concentrating solely on work and spending our spare time indulging in the Sydneysider's real estate obsession, we gravitated to the great outdoors. Dog friendly parks and beaches became our new destinations.

Minou and I have forged a very special relationship over the past 11 years. She's always been my rock—the one who idolises me, even when everyone else seems disinterested. She has accompanied me on nearly all my television shoots (she even gets fan mail!) and together we've worked towards helping others take advantage of the special kind of therapy a dog can offer. Minou and I visited hospitals regularly and we have also visited schools for a 'Pet Pep' awareness program. She's a little star. But it hasn't always been that way. Like all dog owners would know, having a perfect pet takes work, time and understanding on the part of both pet and owner.

When Minou was a puppy, there were plenty of hiccups. She dug up the watering system in the courtyard, drove the neighbours crazy on a few occasions with whining and barking, and had plenty of toilet training 'mishaps'. As a young dog, she was wary of children and even growled at them a few times. With Minou came the opportunity for me to practice what I preach. It's taken many hours of training, exercise routines, positive rewards, research and socialisation but I now have a well-mannered, self-assured dog who is confident and happy in the company of our young kids and also settles happily in our absence. The most important advice I can give anyone considering getting a dog is to do your research. Make sure you choose the right breed of dog and be realistic about the time and money owning a pet entails.

Researching breeds

Aside from the obvious differences in size and coat length and shedding, different breeds of dog have different activity levels and also very different temperaments. The last chapter of the book contains a glossary of dog breeds which outlines some of the personality traits of each breed along with a care guide.

Each year, hundreds of thousands of dogs enter dog shelters. The most common reason for these surrenders is simply that the dog did not fit into the household. The owner's expectations were different from the outcome. I have so many real life examples of clients who chose the wrong breed/type of dog for their situation that I could probably fill a book with that information alone.

Some time ago, I met a family who, seeing the sniffer dogs at the airport, became quite enchanted with Beagles, and decided to get themselves one.

This family was very busy—Dad works long hours and mum stays at home with the three children under five years of age. Two days a week, a nanny looks after the kids while mum is out.

While Charlie was a puppy, things were okay. There were a few toilet incidents, but the breeder had done a pretty good job of getting the toilet training started, and Charlie knew to go on the newspaper. He whined at night, so he was allowed to sleep in the bedroom where he settled down. The kids threw a lot of food scraps at him from the table, but the family was happy enough to have Charlie under the table while they were eating.

When Charlie became a young adult dog, his family brought him to me because they were at their wits' end. Charlie was escaping regularly and barking at visitors. He was obese and was constantly scavenging food. On the rare occasions when they did take him for a walk, he ran off.

What went wrong here? Well, Beagles are great dogs with the right owner, but they are a challenging breed. They need careful obedience training which must be consistent throughout the whole family. They need regular exercise and they are food obsessed (which is why they make such good working dogs) so allowing them to eat from the dinner table, or to beg for food at all, is a recipe for disaster.

In this family, Dad was too tired to train or walk the dog, Mum would walk him sometimes and had tried the odd 'sit' and 'stay' command but found he was too stubborn so just gave up on it, and the nanny really wasn't interested in dogs at all. Before long, Charlie was running his own routine. With no training or entertainment, his instincts took over—eating and escaping become his focus. Charlie was lucky. His pedigree and food obsession landed him a permanent job with lodgings at the quarantine service. For many other dogs who have scored the wrong owners, the end result is a place on death row at the local animal shelter.

There are hundreds of other examples. The elderly frail couple who decided to get another large breed of dog simply because 'they've always had big dogs' only to find they can't take this dog for a walk for fear of being pulled over or having their shoulder dislocated. The family who purchased a poodle cross breed dog because they thought it would be non-shedding, and therefore suitable for their asthmatic child, only to find that this dog had inherited the coat type of whatever dog it had been crossed with, resulting in heavy moulting. These situations often end up in tragedy with the dog needing rehoming.

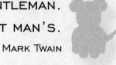

THE DOG IS A GENTLEMAN.
I HOPE I GO TO HIS HEAVEN, NOT MAN'S.

MARK TWAIN

Questions to ask

Before you do anything, make yourself a promise that you won't buy any pet on a whim—and while we're on the subject, NEVER get a puppy as a Christmas present for someone either, let them do the research and make their own decision. Then sit down and answer the following questions:

- How much spare time do you have to devote to a dog?
- Do you live in a house or an apartment?
- Are there any other tennants in the house?
- How many members of the household/family?
- Any allergies?
- Are you active/sporty or mostly an indoors person?
- Are there any other pets in the household?
- How many hours a week do you work?
- How much can you afford to spend on your pet on a weekly basis?
- Do you travel a lot?
- Is your house fully fenced?
- Do the neighbours have dogs/cats?
- Are you emotionally, financially, and personally ready to take on the responsibility of having a new pet?
- Do you understand the nutritional, housing, and health requirements of this pet?
- Have you acquired the necessary items needed to take care of this pet, and have you 'pet-proofed' your house?

- Do you know what type of pet you want, e.g. species, breed, or size, temperament, gender, age, energy level? Write down the characteristics you are looking for. We have heard many stories of people who went to a shelter with one type of pet in mind, and 'fell in love' with an entirely different type of animal, and adopted it. Sometimes this works out fine; other times, the owner regrets the on-the-spur-of-the-moment decision. Be sure to think carefully about what type of pet you are looking for.
- Are all of the family members in agreement about getting a new pet?
- Have guidelines been set for the feeding, grooming, discipline and training, and cleaning up after the pet?

Once you have this information, you should be able to work out which breeds might be suitable for you by looking at the breed profiles in this book.

Don't forget your local vet as a good source of information and also try the breed associations of the relevant breed.

The best website I have found on selecting the right breed is the Pet Care Information and Advisory Service website at www.petnet.com.au. This site has loads of tips and hints and also has a good quiz called the select-a-pet quiz, which will give you a few instant, breed options compatible with your answers.

2

THE SEARCH BEGINS

Once you have decided on the type of dog you want, it's time to contact breeders, pet shops or the welfare shelters. Sometimes your pet will be available immediately, but other times you can expect to be added to a waitlist, which might take several months.

As to where to get the puppy from, you really need to get some local information to make an educated decision. Your vet will have a good idea of the reputation of pet shops in the area. Breeders that are part of their breed association are generally reliable, as is the RSPCA and other animal welfare shelters.

As a rule, I tell people to stay clear of puppy factories. This is partly for moral reasons, but also because there has been concern recently about the temperament of puppies raised in a very intensive situation, with little human interaction. The imprinting age of dogs, when they form a bond with humans and other animals, is between 4 and 11 weeks of age. Puppies that spend most of their time in the company of other dogs, but not humans, sometimes will interact well with dogs, but never really like human company.

WHAT ABOUT POUND PUPPIES?

Obviously it's difficult to predict the nature of a puppy when the breed isn't known. Staff at animal welfare shelters are well trained in temperament assessments and they will have done the job for you. Every dog and puppy rehomed from reputable shelters undergo thorough temperament assessment, and rest assured, the staff will do everything in their power to be confident of a perfect match.

Not all animal shelters are alike but all can be a source of fine quality pets.

Why are animals in shelters?

Many animals that are in shelters are there because the owners can no longer care for them. This can be for a variety of reasons:

- Owners are moving and cannot take their pet with them.
- Owners have health problems.
- Owners have become incapacitated or died.
- Owners no longer have time for a pet because of changes in their lifestyle—for example, a new baby, ill family member.
- Owners may have other pets that don't get along with this pet.
- Owners may have come to the realisation that they should never have got a pet in the first place.

Other animals may end up in shelters because they are homeless or have come from abusive situations.

Evaluation of animals by a shelter

When a dog is surrendered to a shelter, the staff will do a thorough evaluation. This usually involves obtaining a good history of the dog's prior health and behaviour at its last home, a thorough veterinary examination, and sometimes screening for various diseases such as heartworm. Animals will almost always be desexed, microchipped and vaccinated.

Shelters have staff responsible for carrying out detailed temperament assessments. Any pet which fails these assessments cannot be rehomed. Of course, the degree to which all this can be done very much depends on the resources of the shelter. Sometimes you may have to get more thorough health testing done with your own vet.

Ask the staff at the animal shelter how they evaluate animals that come to them. They will be very happy to discuss this with you. You will probably also be able to get a written copy of any veterinary care to keep as part of your record.

The adoption process

There are usually several steps involved in adopting an animal, whether it be from a shelter, pet shop or a breeder. You will first need to fill out an application form, then go about choosing your new pet. After this, you may experience a waiting (or cooling of) period. Finally you will be asked to sign a 'contract', pay the fee and then you will take your new dog home, sometimes for an initial trial period.

The application

Some things you may need when filling out an application to adopt a pet include:

- Proof of age and permanent residence.
- Pet ownership history including vet records.
- Proof of vaccination and registration of other pets.
- Photographic identification.

Important when choosing a pet

Choosing which puppy or dog to take home can be an overwhelming process, but the key here is to stick to the results of your research. Take your list along with you. If you know you cannot keep up the activity levels required for a kelpie or cattle dog, and you don't have time to groom a Samoyed, then no matter how cute he may look in his cage, you will not be his ideal owner.

It is very difficult to get a good idea of an animal's true characteristics while it is inside a cage. Don't be put off by a dog that looks like the ideal breed, just because he may appear shy or a little timid in the cage. Ask shelter staff for advice on the temperament of the pet. Shelter staff are familiar with animals in their care, and often have a very good idea of each individual personality.

It is important that the whole family, including children and even other dogs if possible, meet the pet. This meeting should take place in a quiet, neutral environment, with shelter staff present.

The waiting period

Many shelters and breeders will have a compulsory 'waiting period' of 24 hours before you can take your pet home. This gives you an opportunity to go home and discuss any concerns with the family, and to make 100 per cent sure you are ready for the commitment. The pet will not be given to anyone else during this time.

Obviously, with breeders, sometimes the waitlist can be quite long. Many people are put off by this, but adopting any animal should not be done on a whim. Waiting gives you plenty of time to think whether you really want a pet.

The adoption contract

Certainly at most animal shelters and with many breeders as well as pet shops, you will be asked to read and sign an adoption contract. This contract might include provisions that you:

- Keep the dog only as a domestic pet (obviously not a fighting pet etc.)
- Provide good housing, nutrition and pet care
- Have the dog speyed/castrated (if this has not already been done).
- Allow post adoption visits by the animal shelter (in more unusual circumstances)
- Have had no history of animal abuse or neglect.

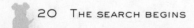

- Will return the animal to the shelter or breeder if you can no longer care for her.
- Have permission from your landlord to keep a pet.
- Understand the shelter/ breeder will take the animal back if it has been mistreated.
- Will pay the associated costs with adopting a pet.
- Have discussed adopting the pet with all family members and they all agree on the pet.

Contracts are not always this involved. It will very much depend on the breeder or animal shelter you go to, and the prior circumstances of the pet you are adopting.

Costs of adoption

In almost all cases you will have to pay an adoption fee for the dog. Some shelters will offer a voucher to help pay for the desexing surgery if this has not already been done.

Trial period

Some shelters may offer a short trial period where you can take the pet home and see how it settles in your environment. Rarely, a minor behavioural or medical problem may be discovered that has not been evident at the shelter. Some shelters will offer assistance in helping you work through these.

Don't rely on a trial period to determine whether a dog is right for you. These periods can be stressful for animals if they are constantly being farmed out from one family to the next. Do your research and avoid having to dislodge animals that you may otherwise have been able to rule out earlier.

Benefits from adopting from shelters

Adopting pets from shelters can have many rewards. Many people say they are happy that they could save the life of a wonderful animal by giving him a new and loving home. The RSPCA 2007/2008 statistics revealed that 70,514 dogs were received by the RSPCA in that year alone, and of these 23,772 had to be euthenased. Shelters are filled with animals which were and could continue to be great pets, as well as animals who, with a little training, can become a cherished member of the family.

Animal shelters provide a wonderful mix of adoptable animals. Some are pure breeds; others are virtually one of a kind. Animals are also of various ages. Many people prefer to have an older pet so there are no surprises about how big he will grow or the type of coat he may have.

Adopting an animal from a shelter is generally less expensive than acquiring an animal through a breeder or pet shop. Of course, you need to remember that the real financial cost of a pet over her lifetime is not her purchase price, but the food, grooming, health care, toys, etc. If you do not have the money to buy an expensive pet, you need to carefully look at your finances to be sure you can afford any pet, and still provide the care he needs.

While it varies with the shelter, you can usually get good information on the temperament and personality of the animal you are interested in. You may even have access to his health records, and a good description of his life in his former home.

Many shelters now neuter and spay all animals before they can be adopted as pets. Others may provide you with a certificate that will pay for a portion of the surgery. Most of the animals would have also been wormed and vaccinated. Most animals will be house trained, and many dogs, for instance, have some basic training.

Myths about animals from shelters

Some people think that all animals in shelters were surrendered because of behavioural problems. This is not true. Many animals in shelters have impeccable behaviour and habits. If the reason the animal was brought to the shelter was a behaviour problem, it may have been more a problem with the previous owner's behaviour than the animal's. Training takes time, patience, and consistency; if the owner is lacking any of these, the animal's behavior will suffer.

Other people believe that you cannot train an adult dog: 'you can't teach old dogs new tricks'. This, too, is untrue. Older animals can easily learn bad habits or good habits; it is up to the owner.

Do adopted shelter animals need special care?

Animals in shelters are undergoing considerable stress. They may not be used to cages or other animals. They are missing their old territory, and in many cases, their loving owner who had to give them up. They may have been moved from their home, to the shelter, and now to a new home all in a very short time. Think of how moving is stressful for you and how hard it is to lose so many familiar things. The animals are experiencing the same thing. They may need extra patience, assurance and guidance. They may need your presence more than other animals who have come into your home.

Bonding with your new pet is very important. Play with her and be with her as she explores her new surroundings.

Having a crate for your new pet is a good idea. You may think, 'but she has been caged in the shelter; I do not want to cage her again.' A cage in your home will be more like a den to your new pet and keep her safe while you are not around to monitor her activities. Some animals may find the space of a whole house overwhelming and find comfort in a small cozy place they can call their own.

Depending upon the physical condition of your new pet, special nutrition may be necessary. Some animals may be too fat, others too thin. Some may have had very poor nutrition in their previous home. Ask the shelter what they fed your new pet and continue feeding that for a week or more as your new pet adjusts. Then if you want to change the diet, do it slowly.

In most cases, the shelter will try to bathe and groom your pet before you receive him. They may have limited time and facilities, however, so you may need to spend more time grooming your pet at first. Make it a happy and fun time. It will be a good time for you to bond with each other.

Take training slowly. Your new pet has a lot of adjustments to make. Train with patience, affection and quiet firmness. Consistency is very important. Be sure you, and all family members, use the same commands in the same manner.

Pound summary

Animal shelters provide an invaluable service of providing safe havens for animals and matching them to new, loving owners. Adopting an animal from a shelter can be a wonderful experience if you are well prepared for a new pet. Shelters are also a great place to volunteer your time. You will be glad you did.

THERE IS NO PSYCHIATRIST IN THE WORLD
LIKE A PUPPY LICKING YOUR FACE.
BEN WILLIAMS

HOW DO I APPROACH A BREEDER?

If you're after a pure breed, then breeders will be the obvious choice. For a list of breeders, contact your local Canine Council or Canine Breeders Association. You will probably find a visit to the breeder a sort of reverse-retail experience. They will often be as wary of you as you are of them.

Far from having a dog pushed on you, you should expect to answer questions about your work, family and lifestyle. Breeders are passionate about their dogs and want them to go to the most appropriate families. They are not in it just for the money and they generally make a life out of breeding and showing their chosen type of dog.

One of my clients sat through a three-hour interview before the breeder was satisfied as to her suitability. This is an extreme example though, and generally, you won't 'fail' the test unless there is an obvious reason.

What about pet shops?

Some pet shops are good, and others are not, so you will need to rely on word of mouth and veterinary advice about the one near you.

A good pet shop will smell clean and the staff will be friendly and knowledgeable about the breed. The puppies should be active, bright eyed, responsive and there should be no sign of diarrhoea in the enclosure.

At a good pet shop, you will not be pressured to make a purchase, in fact, you may be asked to think about your decision overnight and come back the next day if you still feel the same.

Pet shop managers should be able to give you some information on the breeder of the dog they are selling—such as how long they have been breeding dogs, whether they have sold puppies from these breeders before, whether they also breed other dogs and if there have been any problems.

HOW DO I TELL IF THE PUPPY IS HEALTHY?

Selecting a puppy can be a very emotional experience, but you still need to use your common sense. A healthy pup should be active, playful and responsive. Healthy pups have a good, even covering of fat over them. Skinny puppies with rounded bellies often have worms or diarrhoea.

If you choose the tiniest pup shivering in the corner, distancing itself from the others, chances are you have chosen the hard, and possibly expensive road—the pup may be sick and need veterinary treatment. It might be romantic to choose the runt of the litter, but this is not the safe option!

Once you have the puppy out of the enclosure, check it over carefully. There should be no discharge from the eyes or nose. Ears should also be clean (black discharge from ears is a sign of ear mites or infection). The coat should be glossy and healthy looking and the pup should be free of fleas and bald patches (which could indicate ringworm or localized bacterial infections).

What treatments should the puppy have had before I take it home?

Puppies are weaned at around six weeks of age, then rehomed usually between 6 and 12 weeks of age.

They should have been wormed with an intestinal allwormer every two weeks from two weeks of age.

They should be flea-free and treated with a good flea control product.

Puppies should be vaccinated. The usual vaccination routine involves a C3 (distemper, parvovirus, canine infectious hepatitis) or C5 (distemper, parvovirus, infectious canine hepatitis as well as parainfluenza and kennel cough) vaccination at 6 to 8 weeks of age and full C5 vaccination at 12 to 14 weeks of age.

No matter where you purchase your puppy, you should always be given a 48-hour health guarantee-meaning that you can have the dog checked over by a vet in this time, and return it if there are any significant problems.

Heart worm prevention and tick treatment are important in coastal areas especially.

PREPARING MY HOME FOR THE PUPPY

Before puppy comes home, make sure you have the basic things like a dog bed, crate, food and water bowl, collar and lead as well as a few chewy and soft toys.

Make a decision before time on where the puppy will sleep. Ideally it should sleep on its own, in a safe, sheltered environment, away from temptations like power cords and precious furniture.

Allowing a pup to sleep in your room, or, worse still, in bed with you, might be easier (and quieter) at first, but is a recipe for disaster. Puppies need to learn to settle and spend some time each day, and night, alone, so that they don't develop separation anxiety.

The laundry is generally a safe, quiet place. Set up a comfy bed. Food and water bowl, and a radio on low volume as well as some newspaper for toileting needs, and you're set.

As far as feeding is concerned, make sure you have a supply of the same food the puppy has been used to. If you want to change the food, do this gradually, by decreasing the old and increasing the new food over a few weeks. The puppy digestive system is immature and sensitive. Introducing too many new foods quickly will result in diarrhoea. So while Fido may seem to be enjoying his first taste of cabanossi, pizza, bolognaise and Sunday roast, if you give it all at once, I guarantee the first vet visit is going to be sooner than you might have imagined!

Puppy proofing your home

Puppies have a tremendous amount of energy and a natural curiosity. They love to explore the worlds around them. They are also delightfully mischievous and this is what makes them such fun. But it can also lead to disasters and very dangerous situations if these bundles of joy are not supervised. In many ways, having a puppy is just like having an active toddler. Anything that crosses their path is potentially for breaking or eating!

Before you bring your pup home, you should survey the house and garden thoroughly for any potential dangers. This is an involved process but looking on the bright side, it's a jolly good way to have that spring clean out.

Indoors

Puppies will naturally want to inspect all indoor pot plants and have a good chew on them. Put all pot plants out of reach. Some plants such as azaleas and lilies are toxic so you need to be especially diligent with these. It helps to make only certain rooms of your house available to the puppy. This will make the pup proofing process a little less daunting.

- Keep all medications and supplements up high and out of reach. Even if they are in plastic containers, many puppies will chew their way through those.
- Keep the garbage bin out of reach, including the one in the bathroom. Either have it locked in a cupboard or somewhere out of reach. Puppies love the taste and smell of garbage.
- Keep the toilet lid down and don't have sinks or bathtubs full of water in unsupervised areas. It is common for people to have the pup sleeping in the laundry or bathroom while they are toilet training, and many people don't think the dog will try to get into the toilet bowl. Many dogs do this, and not only is it a drowning hazard, but puppies will often eat the toilet bowl fresheners which are usually poisonous.
- Store all your cleaning supplies in a safe cupboard. When you are using sprays and disinfectants, have the puppy out of the way. Puppies like to follow owners around while they are cleaning up, and while it's nice to have company, chemical sprays may land in the puppies' sensitive eyes or the puppies may inhale the vapour of those chemicals.
- Watch out for the puppy around furniture. Pups love to get in,

under things and quite a few toe and leg injuries in young dogs are a result of the puppy sneaking under a rocking chair, or having the leg of a chair or bed land on them.

- It will be impossible to remove all your electrical cords, but if they are chewed through they can cause nasty burns and even electrocution. Tie up what you can, place them in protective piping but most importantly, make sure you provide supervision.
- Check all your curtains to make sure cords are placed up and out of the way, close fireplace grates and keep your clothes and shoes out of reach. Puppies love shoes the most—aside from being a health hazard to them if they end up with an intestinal blockage, a shoe eating habit can be extremely expensive for the owner.
- Any tobacco products, including nicotine patches and gum are potentially fatal to dogs and need to be kept in a secure place.
- Keep all small objects like buttons, coins, little toys and keys as well as jewellery, out of the way.
- Be careful about closing doors as you walk through—your puppy maybe right behind you and get caught.
- Keep doors and windows closed. Keep screens on windows and sliding glass doors securely fastened and in good condition, to keep your puppy from falling through or escaping.
- Close off stairwells with a baby gate.
- Many dogs will relish the chance for a tasty snack out of the cat litter tray. Dogs particularly love cat poo because of its high protein content. For us though, aside from it being a bad habit, eating cat faeces and litter can be a health hazard. Cat litter can cause an intestinal obstruction, and in addition, any intestinal worms the cat has may be passed on to the dog. Place the litter box behind a baby gate, in a separate room or in a closet with the gate across the doorway.

Outdoors

Make sure you inspect your fence carefully before you bring the puppy home, and repair any holes or loose planks to ensure the puppy will not be able to jump over or dig under any part of the fence.

- Never leave your puppy outside without supervision.
- Make a separate area of the garden for the puppy to use as a toilet and make this attractive to him (use sand as a substrate). Fence off any areas where the children play, so he cannot toilet in those (sandpits especially).
- Make sure you fence off or cover ponds, swimming pools and outdoor spas.
- Keep shed doors closed and have fertilizers, chemicals and tools stored safely away.
- Many plants are toxic to animals. Most puppies seem to avoid eating plants that are toxic, so poisoning is not common, but can happen. While it is impossible for most people to re-landscape their gardens, when planting new ones, check with the nursery as to what is poisonous. Some examples include the potato plant, foxglove, daffodil bulbs and oleanders as well as frangipanis. Cocoa bean mulch is also poisonous to dogs. Never use snail bait or rat sac if you have a pet. These are deadly. For snail control, use pet friendly alternatives such as half full beer cans buried in the soil.

How to choose a name for the puppy

Believe it or not, there are some do's and don'ts when it comes to choosing a name for your dog. As a vet, I've seen some of the weirdest and most unusable names you can imagine. It might seem endearing to call your pooch 'Moron', 'Butt Head', 'Queen Victoria' or 'Peepee Doodle' at home, but will you actually call that out in the park?

Here are the rules...

Avoid names that sound like commands. Dogs rely on 'sounds like' rather than meaning. So if you are going to use commands like 'sit', 'come', 'stay', 'drop', 'fetch' or 'heel' you shouldn't call your pet 'Kit', 'Rum', 'Tay' 'Mop' 'Fletch' or 'Teal'. It won't be helpful if every time you call 'Fletch' in the park, he runs off looking for his ball!

Avoid names that sound like someone else's name in the family. This is obviously going to cause confusion.

Keep the name short. This is not only to make it easier for you to shout out in public, but also easier for your pet to understand. We all have the smartest dog in the world, I know, but while humans might understand 'Heavenly Hirani Tiger Lily', your dog (deliberate or not!) is going to forget this one from time to time.

Use 'hard' consonants and vowels in the name. Animals find it much easier to hear the hard sounds such as 'T', 'B', 'C' and 'J' than softer sounds such as 'S', 'M' and 'H'. They also find it easier to hear short, sharp vowel sounds than soft ones. Hence 'Jet', 'Buster' and 'Tilly' are easier for them to hear than 'Lily' and 'Marla'.

Choose a name she can grow into. A cutsey name might suit now, especially if the kids chose it. But just be sure you and the kids will still be happy calling your fully grown rottweiller 'Fluffy Fruit Loops' in a few years' time…

Some popular dog names

Max, Tyke, Buster, Sam, Lucy, Rocky, Daisy, Ginger, George, Jack, Molly, Tilly.

3
THE MEDICAL STUFF

This chapter covers the nuts and bolts of medical stuff you'll encounter in your dog's first year and beyond. While it's very important to have all the routine vaccinations done, and to have a good idea of illnesses and parasites your dog might pick up, please try to stay calm. There is a culture lurking out there that ignorantly hints at our pets being walking vectors of disease.

I have a client who, being a perfectionist and a scientist at heart, took it upon herself to research every possible ailment her new puppy might contract, in the hope that she could take all steps at avoidance and early detection. Unfortunately, the old saying 'a little knowledge is a very dangerous thing' rang true for her. On her first visit, the puppy had a mild bout of diarrhoea. We did the routine in-house faecal tests and in the absence of any worm eggs and parasites in the poo, the dog was diagnosed with the most common form of puppy diarrhoea—dietary indiscretion. During the consult, however, we happened to mention a few possible ailments the owner hadn't heard of before. This must have panicked her, for over the next months, she embarked on a massive research project into all things canine on the internet (to save your own sanity, ask your vet or get a good textbook before you try to decipher right from wrong on the net, PLEASE!)

The poor woman was in week after week, worried that a tiny graze on a foot was demodex mange, that a speck of brownish ear wax might be ear mites or evidence of some rare cyst or tumour lurking within, or that feeding supermarket dry food might have given her dog cancer or 'doggie aids' (which, by the way, doesn't exist).

The final straw was when she came in with the dog concerned that she was not finding fleas on it despite checking thoroughly using various different visual and combing techniques. You see, even though she was applying the correct products with religious regularity, she found an internet site that promises all dogs and cats harboured secret nests of vermin, immune to modern day chemical warfare (garlic and incense were the only real cure, of course!). This client is now content to read all the information handouts we can give her, but she could have made things much easier for herself by just asking her vet for advice in the first place.

What happens at the first vet check?

Once you have purchased your pup, you should have it professionally checked over by your veterinarian. This is rather like a paediatrician's examination of a new born baby.

At this check up, the vet will look for general signs of health as well as any congenital abnormalities (abnormalities it was born with). The vet will usually start at the front of the dog and work backwards, first checking the teeth.

Teeth: Puppies should have 24 temporary (milk) teeth. They should have a scissor bite, with the bottom jaw very slightly shorter than the top, so the teeth interlock. The mouth should be generally clean with no smelliness, discharge or bleeding. Some abnormalities commonly seen include underbite, overbite, base narrow canines, wry bite and missing teeth. These problems are rarely life threatening, but might require some correcting, or may be important if you are wanting to breed from your pet.

Eyes: The vet will check that both eyes are clear and free from discharge, conjunctivitis and infections or ulcers. Common eye abnormalities include:

Entropion: The bottom eyelid turns inwards, resulting in inflammation and infection from hairs rubbing on the eyeball.

Ectropion: The bottom lid droops and turns outwards, causing tears to pool in the lower lid area, and the eyes to weep.

Cherry eye: This is a prolapsed gland inside the lid of the eye which needs surgery to be corrected.

Ears: The ears should be clean and free of any smell. The most common ear conditions are infections or ear mites. Both of these are generally represented by a smelly discharge and the pup will often be shaking its head or even whimper when patted on the head. With ear mites, the discharge is usually black and crusty.

Heart and lungs: This is a very important part of the veterinary examination, particularly as you, the pet owner will not be able to detect any heart abnormalities by just observing the dog. The vet uses a stethoscope to listen to the heart and lungs. The normal heart has a distinctive 'lub-dub' sound. If the vet detects a murmur, the sound will be a swishing, a 'click' or similar. Not all heart murmurs are life threatening or even significant, but many are and if the vet detects a murmur, they may suggest further diagnostic tests such as cardiac ultrasound, radiographs, ECG monitoring or similar. Some important heart problems detected in pups include PDA or patent ductus arteriosis, mitral valve insufficiency and AV septal defects.

Abdomen: The vet will have a good feel of the pups tummy, to ensure the liver, kidneys and spleen are a normal size and also feel the intestines. With male dogs, they will check that there are two testicles. Some dogs will have only one testicle (monorchid) or there may be no testicles descended into the scrotum (cryptorchid). Sometimes the testicles will descend into the scrotum later, as late as six months of age. If they are not in the scrotum by the time the dog is six months old, they will have to be removed surgically because they often become cancerous.

The other important aspect of abdominal examination is checking for hernias. Hernias are holes where the muscles of the abdomen have not knitted together. Very small hernias can be left, but when the hole is large enough for intestinal contents or fat to fall into it, this can be life threatening, so the hernia should be closed early on. There are generally three types of hernias:

Umbilical Hernia: where the dog's belly button is.

Inguinal hernia: in the groin area, where the tummy meets the back leg.

Perineal hernia: a hole between the anal area and the muscles of the bottom.

Skin: The vet will check the skin and coat for fleas, ticks, bald patches and any local infections. Fleas and local infections can be easily treated. On the other hand, if the vet finds evidence of demodex (otherwise known as mange) this can be expensive and time consuming to treat.

Demodex are small mites which live in the hair follicles and skin. They are passed from the mother to the puppy. The mite causes the hair to fall out and causes damage to hair follicles and the skin. The result is hairlessness with bacterial infection. Most of the time, cases can be treated with long courses of antibiotics and insecticides but some cases require life long management and can even be life threatening.

Immune system: The vet will also feel the lymph nodes ('glands') for enlargement and take your pup's temperature. This can sometimes give an indication of whether the puppy may be incubating a virus, or otherwise be feeling unwell.

Making the vet visit easier

If you have one of those dogs that just can't handle visits to the vet, I have a few tips which might help you. First though, take a walk in their paws for a minute and think about what it might be like for them at a veterinary clinic. How would you feel at a doctor's surgery in a foreign country where you didn't speak the language? What would you do to communicate pain or anxiety? Then, how would you react if those poking and prodding you were ten times larger than yourself? Like you, your pet probably feels it is not in control of the situation. In desperation, some animals use aggression to regain some control and if they find it works, they will usually become worse the next time.

Our pets' senses are also different from our own. Their hearing is four times better than ours. Anxiety often leads to noise sensitivity, so pets become jumpy at sounds we can't even detect. A dog's sense of smell is about a thousand times better than ours. A dog can smell fingerprints on glass up to six weeks after we put them there! Couple this with the fact that they are more easily startled by moving objects and find it hard to walk on slippery surfaces and you can just imagine what sort of a place the veterinary clinic must be for your pet.

Vets are quite aware of the problems animals face in their company, and many go to lengths to separate cats and dogs in the waiting room. Some hospitals use a pheromone spray in a plug in diffuser, a feel-good pheromone that naturally calms animals.

There are many things you can do to make your pets visit to the vet a little easier.

- First, remain calm yourself. If you are in control of the situation, your pet will have a much better response.
- If you have a very small breed of dog, you may want to transport it in a cat carrier. Tiny dogs feel safer and calmer when protected in this way.
- Whatever you do, do not do not try to socialize your pet with other animals in the waiting room while it is feeling anxious and upset. Most little dogs don't feel any more comfortable exposed in the path of a rambunctious German Shepherd for example, than we do sitting a metre away from a man-eating crocodile.
- If you know your pet has a difficult time coping with the slippery exam table, you might want to ask the vet to put a towel on it.

- Make sure you come prepared. If you know your dog bites, bring a muzzle or ask the receptionist for one and put it on before the vet arrives. That way, your pet won't get a chance to start any bad behaviour.
- Never ever shout or physically reprimand your pet while it's in this anxious situation. The more calm and quiet everyone is, the better the consult will go.
- Vets are usually well stocked with treats in the consultation room, that you can both give to your pet when it has done a good job.
- Just be wary that you don't reward your pet for bad behaviour. I've been in the situation where an upset dog was having a really good go at biting me, and its distraught owner was desperately trying to ram treats down its throat at the same time! Of course, the owner thought she was distracting the dog but the dog interpreted the treats as a reward for biting!

Finally, there are some animals that will not be calmed by any amount of environmental control or training. For those that do not handle any public situation well and have a tendency towards aggression, consider the help of a veterinary behavioural specialist who will combine training with environmental control and medications as necessary.

A DOG HAS A LOT OF FRIENDS BECAUSE HE WAGS HIS TAIL AND NOT HIS TONGUE.

ANON.

Dentition

Each side of the upper jaw of an adult dog has 3 incisor teeth, 1 large canine tooth, 4 premolars and 2 molar teeth. The lower jaw has 3 incisors, 1 canine tooth, 4 premolars and 3 molars. A dog, therefore, should have 42 permanent teeth. Puppies are born with no teeth but deciduous teeth begin to appear at 3 to 4 weeks of age. In total a puppy will cut 28 'milk' teeth. At about 3 months of age, the permanent teeth will start to erupt and displace the deciduous teeth. By the time the puppy is 7 months old all permanent teeth should be present.

It is vital to maintain a good standard of dental hygiene—nature's way is to give the dog bones to chew and you will never find a dog that has to hunt for his food with bad or dirty teeth. Another way is to brush the dog's teeth regularly using a canine toothpaste. Do not use human toothpaste. Make sure your dog has plenty of suitable things to chew on and this is particularly helpful to him when he is cutting his permanent teeth.

Vaccination

Some canine diseases are very serious and can be fatal even with treatment. To prevent your dog from getting these diseases you should have him vaccinated regularly.

When should I vaccinate?

At 6 to 8 weeks of age puppies should receive their first vaccination; this is temporary and needs to be followed up with another one at 12 weeks. After the 12-week vaccination you can then take your puppy out in public areas. A third vaccination is often necessary and recommended. There are many different vaccination routines out there—they depend largely on the type of vaccination your puppy has had.

What do I need to vaccinate against?

Parvovirus: a highly contagious viral gastroenteritis. Parvovirus is a painful, deadly viral disease of puppies. Although we have been routinely vaccinating against it for some time, it is a relatively new disease (first found in Australia the '70s) so it will be some time before we eradicate it. Signs of parvo include depression, loss of appetite, severe vomiting and diarrhoea containing blood. Death can occur very quickly, even with treatment which often involves several weeks of hospitalisation, intravenous fluid therapy, plasma transfusions and antibiotics as well as pain relief.

Distemper: a highly contagious disease producing symptoms such as conjunctivitis, nasal discharge, convulsive seizures and spinal cord damage. Treatment is often ineffective. This disease is becoming quite uncommon, thanks to vaccination.

Hepatitis: in puppies can cause sudden death, whilst adult dogs can experience, weakness, fever, diarrhoea, loss of appetite and bleeding.

Canine cough: a complex disease caused by bacterium and a virus. The virus is of the same class as the human 'whooping cough'. Affected adult dogs will have a hacking cough persisting for weeks. In puppies and old dogs the disease can be devastating. This disease is sometimes erroneously referred to as 'kennel cough' giving the impression that it is transmitted only in kennels. Far from true. Kennel cough is an airborne disease and can be transmitted at the local park, in communal water bowls and anywhere your pet sees another dog.

Intestinal parasites (worms)

What are tapeworms and roundworms?

Tapeworms and roundworms are two of the most common intestinal parasites of dogs. Tapeworms are long flat worms composed of many individual segments whereas round worms are much shorter and have rounded bodies. Roundworms produce microscopic eggs which are shed in the faeces of infected dogs, whereas tapeworms release mature segments (which again contain eggs) from the end of the worm into the faeces. These segments sometimes look like grains of rice and are mobile. They can occasionally be seen on the hair around the anus of the dog or in the faeces.

How can my dog get roundworms?

Roundworms are very common in young dogs and puppies. The two most common species are *toxocara cati* and *toxascaris leonine*. Infected dogs pass the eggs in their faeces, and when eaten by another dog, the infection is passed on.

There are other methods of transferal: rats and rodents can also be infected and act as the 'intermediate host', transmitting the infection to the dog when they are eaten.

Roundworms can also be transported from the mother to her puppies through her milk.

From earlier infections with roundworms, a bitch will have some larvae remaining dormant in certain tissues in the body and when she gives birth to a litter of puppies these larvae migrate to the mammary glands and are excreted in the milk. This process causes no harm to the mother, but means that puppies are commonly infected with roundworms from a very young age. Roundworm infections are *extremely* common, and it is safe to assume that *all* puppies will be infected.

How can my dog get tapeworms?

There are a variety of different tapeworms that can infect dogs, but the two most common are *dipylidium caninum* and *taenia taeniaformis*. The eggs of the diphylidium tapeworm are shed in the faeces of the infected dog. These eggs are then eaten by the flea larvae. The flea then infests another dog and passes the tapeworm infection to that dog when the dog eats the flea during grooming. You should assume your dog also has tapeworm if it has fleas.

In contrast, the eggs of *taenia taeniaformis* are eaten by rodents (rats and mice) so other dogs become infected during hunting by eating an infected rodent. Infection with this worm is less common therefore, but should be expected in any dog that actively hunts.

Hookworms and whipworms

The other major intestinal worms in dogs are the hookworm and whipworm. The hookworm can cause severe intestinal bleeding and anaemia in puppies. The worm attaches to the lining of the gut wall, using its teeth to damage the wall, then feeding off the tissues. The eggs are then shed in the faeces. Hookworm larvae can also penetrate the skin causing an itchy dermatitis. The larvae can be passed from the mother in her milk.

Whipworms burrow into the large intestine and large burdens of this worm can cause a bloody, mucous-filled diarrhoea.

Can these worms infect humans?

It is possible for humans to be infected with both roundworms and tapeworms. Tapeworm infection is very rare however, as it requires ingestion (eating) of an infected flea. Roundworm is more of a concern, particularly in children, where ingestion of the eggs may result in migration of the worm larvae through the body.

Due to the potential human health hazard, as well as the possible ill-health to the dog, regular worming of dogs is important. In addition, careful disposal of faeces is important.

What should I use to worm my puppy, and when?

A variety of products are available to treat worms in dogs but they are *not* all equally effective. For the best advice on the type of worming preparation most suitable for your pup, ask your vet. I recommend puppies be given Sentinal Spectrum monthly as it treats all intestinal worms as well as heartworm, and stops flea eggs from hatching. Clients find this the most straightforward program.

As puppies can be infected with roundworms from a very young age it is important that worming is started early and repeated regularly. Tapeworms are more likely to be a problem in adult dogs and at this age less frequent but still regular worming is required. A good worming protocol for puppies is:

- Use an allwormer every two weeks until the pup is 12 weeks of age, then worm monthly until six months of age, then every three months.

Coccidiosis

Coccidia are small protozoans that live in the intestinal tracts of dogs and cats. They cause disease most commonly in puppies and kittens less than 6 months of age, in adult animals whose immune system is suppressed, or in animals who are stressed in other ways (e.g.; change in ownership, other disease present).

As a puppy grows, he tends to develop a natural immunity to the effects of coccidia. As an adult, he may carry coccidia in his intestines, and shed the cyst in the faeces, but experience no ill effects.

How are coccidia transmitted?

A puppy is not born with the coccidia organisms in his intestine. However, once born, the puppy is frequently exposed to his mother's faeces, and if the mother is shedding it in her faeces, then the young animals will likely ingest them and coccidia will develop within the young animal's intestines. Since young puppies, have no immunity to coccidia, the organisms reproduce in great numbers and parasitize the young animal's intestines. Sometimes this causes severe disease.

From exposure to the coccidia in faeces to the onset of the illness is about 13 days. Most puppies who are ill from coccidia are, therefore, two weeks of age and older. Although most infections are the result of spread from the mother, this is not always the case. Any infected puppy or kitten is contagious to other puppies or kittens.

What are the symptoms of coccidiosis?

The primary sign of an animal suffering with coccidiosis is diarrhoea. The diarrhoea may be mild to severe depending on the level of infection. Blood and mucous may be present, especially in advanced cases. Severely affected animals may also vomit, lose their appetite, become dehydrated, and in some instances, die from the disease.

Most infected puppies I have encountered are in the 4 to 12-week age group. The possibility of coccidiosis should always be considered when a loose stool or diarrhoea is encountered in this age group. A microscopic fecal exam by a veterinarian will detect the cysts confirming a diagnosis.

Stress plays an important role in the development of coccidiosis. It is not uncommon for a seemingly healthy puppy to arrive at his new home and develop diarrhoea several days later leading to about 13 of coccidia. If the puppy has been at the new home for less than thirteen days, then he had coccidia before he arrived.

Remember, the incubation period (from exposure to illness) is about 13 days. If the puppy has been with his new owner several weeks, then the exposure to coccidia most likely occurred after the animal arrived at the new home.

What are the risks?

Although many cases are mild, it is not uncommon to see severe, bloody diarrhea result in dehydration and even death. This is most common in animals who are ill or infected with other parasites, bacteria, or viruses. Coccidiosis is very contagious, especially among young puppies. Entire kennels may become contaminated, with puppies of many age groups simultaneously affected.

What is the treatment of coccidiosis?

Fortunately, coccidiosis is treatable. Most of the drugs used work by stopping the ability of the protozoa to reproduce, so time is allowed for the puppy's own immunity to develop and remove the organisms. Drug treatments of one to three weeks are usually required.

If your puppy has coccidia you will also need to take measures to ensure he cannot reinfect himself through his environment. Make sure all faeces are removed immediately. Provide clean food and water at all times.

Throw out any infected bedding, or clean it by boiling it. Keep the dog's home clear of cockroaches and flies which can spread the disease. Coccidia of dogs and cats cannot be transmitted to humans.

Flea control

Fleas are one of the most upsetting topics a dog owner has to endure. Many time pet owners will react as though you have slapped them across the face if you tell them their pet has fleas.

If your pet has fleas, it doesn't mean you keep a filthy household or a negligent pet owner. It's rather like children and head lice—your dog is likely to pick up fleas at least once in his lifetime.

If you have good control methods in place it will never be a big problem. Below is the best information to equip you for controlling fleas.

What should I do to kill the fleas on my dog?

This is a simple question with a rather complex answer. Successful flea control has two aspects. Fleas must be controlled on your dog, and fleas must be controlled in your dog's environment. Since dogs and cats share the same fleas, the presence of a cat in your dog's environment makes flea control much more difficult.

To appreciate the complex issue of flea control, you must understand something about the life cycle of the flea.

Fleas seem to be rather simple creatures. How complicated can their life cycle be?

Although you are only able to see the adult flea, there are actually four stages of the life cycle. The adult flea constitutes only about five per cent of the entire flea population if you consider all four stages of the life cycle. Flea eggs are pearly white and about 0.5mm (1/32in) in length. They are too small to see without magnification. Fleas lay their eggs on the dog, but the eggs do not stick to the dog's hair. Instead, they fall off into the dog's environment. The eggs make up 50 per cent of the flea population. They hatch into larvae in 1 to 10 days, depending on temperature and humidity. High humidity and temperature favour rapid hatching. Flea larvae are slender and about 2 to 5mm (1/8 to 1/4in) length. They feed on organic debris found in their environment and on adult flea faeces, which is essential for successful development.

They avoid direct sunlight and actively move deep into carpet fibres or under organic debris (grass, branches, leaves, or soil). They live for 5 to 11 days and then pupate. Moisture is essential for the survival of these immature stages of the flea; larvae are killed by drying. Therefore, it is unlikely that they survive outdoors in shade-free areas. Outdoor larval development occurs only where the ground is shaded and moist and where flea-infested pets spend a significant amount of time. This allows flea faeces to be deposited in the environment. In an indoor environment, larvae survive best in the protected environment of carpet or in cracks between hardwood floors. They thrive in warm conditions.

Following complete development, the mature larvae produce a silk-like cocoon in which the next step of development, the pupa, resides. The cocoon is sticky, so it quickly becomes coated with debris from the environment. This serves to camouflage it. In warm, humid conditions, pupae become adult fleas in 5 to 10 days. However, the adults do not emerge from the cocoon unless stimulated by physical pressure, carbon dioxide, or heat.

Pre-emerged adult fleas can survive up to 140 days within the cocoon. During this time, they are resistant to insecticides applied to their environment. Because of this, adult fleas may continue to emerge into the environment for up to 3 months following insecticide application. When the adult flea emerges from its cocoon, it immediately seeks a host because it must have a blood meal within a few days to survive. It is attracted to people and pets by body heat, movement, and exhaled carbon dioxide. It seeks light, which means that it migrates to the surface of the carpet so that it can encounter a passing host. Following the first blood meal, female fleas begin egg production within 36 to 48 hours. Egg production can continue for as long as 100 days, which means that a single flea can produce thousands of eggs. This entire life cycle (adult flea → egg → larva → pupa → adult) can be completed in 7 to 21 days with the proper temperature and humidity conditions. This adds to the problem of flea control.

What can these fleas do to my dog?

If untreated, the female flea will continue to take blood for several weeks. During that time, she will consume about 15 times her body weight in blood. Although the male fleas do not take as much blood, they, too, contribute to significant blood loss from the host animal. This can lead to the dog having an insufficient number of red blood cells, which is known as anaemia. In young or debilitated dogs, the anaemia may be severe enough to cause problems. Contrary to popular belief, most dogs do not itch too much due to fleas. However, many dogs become allergic to the saliva in the flea's mouth. When these dogs are bitten, intense itching occurs, causing the dog to scratch and chew continuously.

What can I do to rid my dog of fleas?

Successful flea control must rid the dog of fleas and it must rid the dog's environment of fleas. In fact, environmental control is probably more important than what is done to the dog. If your dog remains indoors and you do not have other pets that come in from the outside, environmental control is relatively easy. However, the dog that goes outdoors or stays outdoors presents a significant challenge. It may be impossible to completely rid the environment of fleas under these conditions, though flea control should still be attempted. When the dog is free-roaming or other dogs are allowed access to the dog's garden, the task of flea control becomes even more difficult.

What can I do for my dog?

Many insecticides that are applied to the dog have limited effectiveness against fleas because they are only effective for a few hours after application. Also, most of these products are effective only against adult fleas. Flea powders, sprays and shampoos will kill the fleas present on your dog at the time of application. However, most of these products have little or no residual effects, so the fleas that return to your dog from the environment are not affected. Thus, your dog may be covered with fleas within a day after having a flea bath or being sprayed or powdered. There are some newer, more effective sprays that can be a valuable part of the overall treatment plan. They kill adult fleas rapidly and are safe enough to use daily, if necessary. Flea sprays containing insect growth regulators are helpful in managing the overall problem because they help to break the flea life cycle. Some of the newer pet sprays with growth regulators are not recommended for daily use; once weekly application is sufficient. Always read the label when using any new flea product on a dog. Recently many more sophisticated products have become available that not only have a high knock-down effect i.e. killing adult fleas on the animal, but also have long residual effects. Some require repeat applications only every several weeks. Tablets, spot on and pour on preparations are all available today. Remember these products will not kill fleas that have not emerged from their cocoon.

Please consult your vet. For example, some dogs with sensitive skins are irritated by flea collars and these should not be worn.

What can I do to minimize fleas in the environment?

Environmental flea control usually must be directed at the dog's immediate environment, the house and any outbuildings occupied by the dog. Even though fleas may be in your house, they are usually never seen. Fleas greatly prefer dogs and cats to people—they only infest humans when there has not been a dog or cat in the house for several days, there are exceptions to this. You may have the house professionally fumigated or use a spray with a long residual effect.

I have heard that there is a once monthly flea tablet available. Is that true?

Yes. This product is given once monthly, but it is important to understand what it does and does not do. It does not have any effect on adult fleas; to kill them, you must use the other products that have been mentioned. The monthly product causes the female fleas to lay abnormal eggs that do not hatch. This means that you will not see results for 1 to 4 months, depending on the number of fleas present. Since fleas live all the year round in our warm centrally heated houses, it is important that the product is used regularly. Control of the entire flea population is then possible especially when combined with one of the environmental products to kill adult fleas. One of the advantages of the product is that it appears to be particularly non-toxic, both to our pets and ourselves.

I have not seen fleas on my dog. Does that mean that none are present?

When a dog is heavily infested with fleas, it is easy to find them. If the numbers are small, it is best to quickly turn your dog over and look on its belly. If you do not find them there, look on the back just in front of the tail. Be sure to part the hair and look at the level of the skin. When the numbers are very small, look for 'flea dirt'. Flea dirt is faecal matter from the flea that contains digested blood. Finding flea dirt is a sure indication that fleas are present or have been present recently. Flea dirt looks like pepper. It varies from tiny black dots to tubular structures about ½mm (¹/₃₂in) long. If you are in doubt of its identification, put the suspected material on a light coloured table top or counter top. Add one or two drops of water, and wait about 30 seconds. If it is flea dirt, the water will turn reddish brown as the blood residue goes into solution. Another method is to put some of the material on a white paper towel and then wet the paper towel with water. A red stain will become apparent if you gently wipe the material across the surface of the paper towel. Many people find tiny drops of blood in a dog's bedding or where the dog sleeps. This is usually flea dirt that was moistened, then dried. It leaves a reddish stain on the bedding material and is another sign that fleas are present.

I just got my dog home from boarding and it has fleas. Doesn't that mean that they were picked up while boarding?

Not necessarily. If you recall, pre-emerged adult fleas can survive up to 140 days within the cocoon. This is significant when your pets are gone from home for extended periods of time. During the time that the house is quiet and empty, pre-emerged adults remain in their cocoon. Even if the house was treated with an insecticide, their cocoon protects them. When people and pets return to the house, adults emerge from their cocoons and immediately begin to seek a blood meal. They jump on dogs, cats, and even people. Although it may appear that a dog just returned from boarding brought fleas to your home, it is also very possible that a sudden emergence of adult fleas may account for the fleas present. Do not be too quick to blame the kennels, after all they do not want fleas any more than you do and any reputable boarding kennel will have rigorous flea control anyway.

Heartworm

Heartworms are capable of causing severe disease and death in dogs. In areas where heartworm is endemic, continuous and preventative medication is needed to prevent the establishment of heartworm and avoid heartworm disease. It is better to prevent heartworm disease because heartworm is fatal to the dog and treatment is costly.

What is a heartworm?

Heartworm (*dirofilaria immitis*) is commonly found in the right chamber of the heart, the pulmonary artery (which is the main artery leaving the right chamber of the heart going into the lungs) and the vena cava (which is the main vein entering the right chamber collecting blood from the rest of the body). Heartworms are generally about 12 to 30cm long (up to 12in).

Life cycle of the heartworm

It is important to understand the life cycle of the dog heartworm to prevent the disease from taking hold. Mosquitoes spread heartworm. A mosquito bites an infected dog, and picks up the heartworm larvae, then bites an uninfected dog, and while it is feeding from the dog's blood, it injects the heartworm larvae into the dog's bloodstream. The larvae mature as they migrate through the bloodstream, through the vessels of the lungs and into the heart. By the time they have reached the heart, the worms have matured into adults. This process takes about 6 months. The adult female heartworm will then lay live young (called microfilaria) which circulate around the bloodstream, ready to be picked up by the next mosquito, and spread to the next dog.

Dog heartworm symptoms

The symptoms of heartworm can take months to years to develop after the dog has become infected. Most of the effects on the body occur from the heartworm larvae travelling through the blood vessels of the lungs, heart and liver. They cause a great deal of irritation as they do so. Most of the time, the first sign of heartworm will be a mild cough, which often goes unnoticed by owners. This then develops into a more serious cough, as well as exercise intolerance, tiredness and breathing difficulties. If left untreated, dogs may develop heart failure or liver failure and many die.

Heartworm control

The cornerstone to prevention of heartworm is firstly to give a preventative medication and secondly to control mosquitoes in the environment.

There are many forms of heartworm prevention, from daily or monthly tablets, to spot on chemicals that are applied to the skin, or an annual injection that can be done along with annual vaccinations. All these treatments are safe and effective as long as you keep up to date.

If a treatment has lapsed, you will need to have a blood test done to be sure your dog hasn't contracted the disease.

Mosquito control in the environment

Because heartworm needs mosquitoes in order to spread, dogs in areas where there are no mosquitos don't have heartworm. If you are in a mosquito area, use repellents, citronella and make sure you get rid of any stagnant water, or use mosquito dunks to rid ponds of mozzies.

Tick paralysis

The two most common ticks found on dogs are the paralysis tick and the brown dog tick. The paralysis tick is by far the most dangerous of the two. The paralysis the tick causes can become evident in many different ways, but usually causes a wobbliness of the gait, followed by collapse in the hind limbs, and then the front legs. Sometimes the first symptoms will be a change in the bark, or difficulty breathing. Paralysis ticks are deadly. Prevention is much better than cure.

Where are paralysis ticks found?

These ticks need a warm, humid climate to survive and to breed. They will not live in cold, dry environments.

How do I search for a paralysis tick?

Ticks are notoriously difficult creatures to find. If you live in the 'tick belt' or are staying in a tick area, you will need to search your pet every day. Keeping the pets coat short will help to make the search easier.

Most (around 70 per cent) ticks are located on the pet's face and muzzle area but it is important to search the entire dog. It is easier to use your fingers to 'feel' the tick than to try and see it. With your fingers, gently work through the coat and check for any suspicious lumps. Part the fur, and have a good look at any lumps you might find. Ticks are a greenish grey in colour. The legs of the paralysis tick are all bunched up at the head region, not spread along the body. This distinguishes them from other ticks.

How do I remove the tick?

There is debate about this but from experience, I feel the best way to remove the tick is to pull it out quickly and confidently with a pair of tweezers, or with your fingers. Don't gently squeeze it, or fiddle with it as this might cause more toxin to be injected into your pet.

Don't fret if you have left the head of the tick in the skin. Once its body has been removed, it is a dead tick and will no longer be able to cause any harm. At worst, the head might cause a little pimple to form.

Once you have removed the tick, put it in a jar and take it, and your pet, straight to the vet. The vet will examine the pet for signs of tick paralysis that you may not have picked up, and also do a thorough search for any more ticks and probably apply a tick treatment.

If your pet is showing signs of tick paralysis, it may need to be admitted to hospital for antitoxin to be administered. Antitoxin does not reverse the signs of tick paralysis but it prevents any further toxin from binding to the nerve receptors, so the condition will hopefully not get worse. In some cases, when animals are severely affected, pets will need to spend several day on a ventilator, being given fluid therapy, having their lungs kept clear and their bodies supported while they metabolize the toxin.

Signs of tick paralysis

The most common sign is a weakness and wobbliness of the back legs, followed by a paralysis in the hind, where the dog will drag itself along by the front legs. Other signs can also occur though, including a cough, difficulty breathing, extreme anxiety and panting, a change in bark, or vomiting.

Preventing ticks

The best way to prevent ticks is to use a vet recommended prevention product. Combining oral and topical products is a good idea.

Keep your pet's coat nice and short and avoid known areas that are known to be heavily infested with ticks.

Should I have my pet desexed?

Desexing or sterilizing male and female dogs is important for several reasons. Not only does it prevent bitches coming into season (oestrus) but it also prevents unwanted litters and has many positive behavioural benefits. Desexed pets are less likely to roam and get into fights, are less likely to suffer from aggression and also less inclined to spend all their 'outdoor' time marking their territory by (sometimes embarrassingly) peeing on anything that resembles a tree trunk. Desexed pets are also protected from many potentially life-threatening health problems, such as pyometra (infection of the uterus) and prostate cancer. Dogs can be desexed as early as eights weeks of age, but the generally accepted ideal age to do the procedure is six months.

What happens to my dog when it is admitted to hospital for its desexing surgery?

Every pet owner has some anxiety about leaving their pet for the day at the vet. It can be as traumatic as leaving your child at daycare for the first time. Fido usually isn't too keen on staying either. Some animals have to be coaxed into staying, kicking and screaming, torn away from their owners, and taken to a foreign environment.

While this procedure definitely tugs at the heartstrings, think of what the childcare workers told you when you picked your child up after he has exhibited anxiety on drop off. Usually the child gets through the doors and settles straightaway, content to join in on the goings on, and reassured by their carers. It's pretty much the same for our dogs. They are usually reluctant to come into the hospital, but once they are there, most settle quickly.

Many pet owners find it reassuring if they can see the environment their pet will stay in, and if they can be given a timetable of his day.

Here is an outline of what happens to your dog when it is admitted for a routine spey or castration operation.

You will be asked to fast the dog the night before surgery. He/she will be allowed to have water, but no food should be given after nine or 10pm. This is to minimize the risk of vomiting and aspirating the vomit (breathing it in) while the dog is under anaesthetic.

Admissions for surgery are early in the morning (generally before 9am). You should take your pet for a short walk before he arrives, to give him an opportunity to go to the toilet.

During the admission procedure, the nurse will weigh your pet and ask you some questions about whether he/she has been fasted, whether there have been any illnesses recently, and also if you want to have a pre anaesthetic blood test done. I'll explain what a pre anaesthetic blood test is later in this chapter, but for the record, I would recommend you have it done if you can afford it. At our hospital, this test has saved quite a few lives.

Once you have signed the admission papers (giving the vet permission to perform the surgery) your pet will be escorted through to the hospital. You are quite welcome to request to see where he will be staying, but it is usually best to make this brief, so Fido can settle quickly.

Animals are put into secure cages appropriate for their size. This is not dissimilar to their crate at home, if they have one—a crate trained animal usually settles very happily in hospital. Soft bedding is provided.

After a short time, the nurse and vet will do a thorough clinical examination. This involves listening to the heart, taking the temperature, pulse, palpating the abdomen and generally looking over the dog. At this time, blood will be collected for a pre anaesthetic test, if it has been requested. The nurse or vet will also calculate dose rates for the pre anaesthetic medication and the injectable anaesthetic (induction agent) and will record this on the dog's anaesthetic chart.

Approximately 30 minutes prior to surgery, the pre anaesthetic sedation will be administered. This is generally given as an injection under the skin or into the vein and is given for several reasons: to provide immediate pain relief, support the heart rate and blood pressure during the surgery, make the recovery more smooth and gentle and to minimize the amount of induction agent that needs to be used. Animals are quite often routinely placed on intravenous fluids during surgery—this also supports their blood pressure and circulation.

Once the premed takes effect, the dog will be drowsy but still awake.

Now, it is given an anaesthetic induction agent to anaesthetize it. This is sometimes an intravenous drug, and sometimes a mask will be placed over the muzzle for the dog to breathe in a gas.

Once your dog is asleep, the vet will pass a tube down its throat. This is called an endotracheal tube. The tube is hooked up to the anaesthetic machine which provides a constant flow of oxygen as well as the anaesthetic gas (the most common being one called isoflurane). At this time, various monitors may be used to keep track of your pet's blood pressure, temperature, pulse and heart rate. The dog will be taken into the surgery, a sterile room, for the surgical procedure to be performed.

Dog spey

This is the sterilization procedure performed on the female dog, where both the ovaries and the uterus is removed. Even though this surgery is quite routine, it is still a challenging procedure. The blood vessels to the ovary and uterus can be very large and friable. Many of my clients ask why the uterus cannot be removed and the ovaries left, or even why we just don't 'tie their tubes'. The answer to this is simple-if the ovaries are left in place, the dog will still come into season every 6 months or so—even though she can't get pregnant, she will still show all the signs of a season (swollen vulva and bleeding) and will be pursued by male dogs, who will attempt to mate with her.

Dog castration

This involves the removal of both testicles. The idea of the castration operation is not only to stop the dog from being fertile, but also to curb any overtly male behaviour. Castrated dogs are less likely to roam, get into fights, and are generally not interested in pestering female dogs. The testicles have to be removed—vascectomies are not performed on dogs routinely.

Once the surgery is complete, your pet will be taken off the anaesthetic machine. Once this happens he will start breathing air and gradually wake up. When he is awake enough to start swallowing, the tube will be removed from his throat and he can be placed back into his hospital cage. He/she will spend the afternoon recovering, and the nurses and vet regularly check on the temperature, breathing and heart rate. He will also receive pain relief injections. Later in the afternoon, the dogs are usually taken for a walk and given a drink of water. Usually no food is given until they get home, in case the pup vomits in the car.

Over the next few days you will need to keep your pet quiet and monitor the wound for any swelling or redness. If your pet chews at the wound, he/she may need to wear an Elizabethan collar. This is like a custom designed 'bucket' that prevents animals chewing at a surgical site. Sutures are generally removed 10 days after surgery.

Below I have included a copy of the post operative handout we give our clients at the hospital.

Post-operative instructions for dogs

What should I do when my dog arrives home after its operation?

On arriving home you should keep your pet warm and comfortable by providing a soft clean bed, ideally in a quiet and draught free room at approximately 20 to 22°C (68 to 72°F). Unless otherwise instructed, your dog should be offered a drink of fresh water. After a few hours a small amount of food may be given, such as white fish or boiled or grilled chicken. Please keep your dog indoors overnight, or longer if instructed, and allow the use of a litter tray. You should discourage any jumping or activity that will cause excessive stretching of the wound, especially during the first few days post-operatively.

My dog seems very sleepy, is this normal?

Your dog has been given a general anaesthetic and/or a sedative. These drugs can take a number of hours to wear off and may cause some patients to appear drowsy for a day or so. Over the next day or two their behaviour should return to normal, however if you are at all concerned do not hesitate to contact the surgery. Most dogs sleep even more than normal in the first week after surgery.

Why has my dogs foreleg been clipped?

This is where the anaesthetic or sedative was administered. There may also be a small dressing on the leg; if so this can be removed the following day unless otherwise instructed.

My dog has developed a slight cough since the operation. Is this anything to worry about?

Your dog may have had a tube placed in their trachea (windpipe) during the anaesthetic. This can occasionally cause mild irritation and a slight cough. If so, it will settle down over the next few days, however should it persist then contact the surgery.

What should I do if my dog is licking its wound or chewing the stitches?

It is only natural that your dog may try to clean the operation site, however, if this becomes excessive, then there is a danger of the stitches being pulled out or infection being introduced into the wound. If you have been given an Elizabethan-type collar to prevent the dog chewing then please ensure it is used, otherwise please contact the surgery and ask for one. Not surprisingly, many dogs find these collars strange at first and will attempt to remove them. However, after a short period most animals will settle and tolerate wearing the collar. Once accustomed, it is better to keep the collar on permanently, rather than to take it on and off. Remember—it only takes a few seconds of unobserved chewing for a dog to undo its stitches. If your dog does succeed in removing any of its stitches then call the surgery as soon as possible.

What should the wound look like, and when should I be concerned?

The wound should normally be clean with the edges together and the skin a normal or slightly reddish/pink colour. In pale skinned dogs bruising may be seen around the wound. This may not appear until a few days after the operation, and in some cases can seem excessive in comparison to the size of the incision, however this is due to seepage of blood under the skin edges. In some cases a small amount of blood may seep intermittently from a fresh wound for up to 24 hours, especially if the animal is active. Contact the surgery if you see any of the following at the wound:

- Continuous seepage or a large quantity of blood.
- Intermittent blood seepage continuing for more than 24 hours.
- Any swellings, excessive redness of the skin or discharge.

When do the stitches need removing?

In general most skin stitches (also called sutures) are removed 7 to 14 days after the operation depending on the type of surgery performed. You will be instructed when is the most appropriate time for your dog.

When can my dog resume a normal active life?

This will depend upon the nature of the operation. In the case of a minor procedure involving a small incision, some restriction of exercise should be maintained until a few days after the skin stitches are removed. However, if major operation has been performed or a large incision is present a longer period of convalescence will be required, which may involve keeping your dog house-bound for a number of weeks.

If you have been given any medication. Please **READ THE LABEL**

CAREFULLY and ensure that all medication is administered as instructed. If you are experiencing any difficulty in dosing your dog contact the surgery for advice.

Pre anaesthetic blood tests

Most veterinary hospitals will offer pre anaesthetic blood testing. This is when a blood and urine sample are taken from your pet and analyzed. Even in a healthy animal, where the vet's clinical exam reveals no sign of disease, there can be some problem that will only be hinted at on an abnormal blood test.

There are countless possible disease processes that affect the way we manage general anaesthetics and sedations, that might show up on blood tests. Some diseases might not affect the anaesthetic, but may be life threatening and the blood test is a good opportunity to discover these early. Pre anaesthetic blood tests are often an 'optional extra' when your pet has an anaesthetic. This is because many people don't want them if they think their pet is healthy. My advice is, if there is any way you can afford it, have it done.

Like all vets, I have encountered many situations where a blood test before an anaesthetic has saved the life of a pet. One seemingly healthy dog came in for a dental scale and polish, only to have his blood results hint at a cancer in his abdomen. An ultrasound revealed that he did have a small tumour, but luckily it was detected early, and he was completely cured after having it surgically removed.

A few examples of conditions that vets commonly discover during pre anaesthetic blood tests include:
- Kidney disease/chronic renal failure
- Diabetes and other hormonal diseases such as Cushings disease and Addisons disease (abnormalities of the pituitary and adrenal gland)
- Anaemia

- Infections, viral or bacterial
- Tumours

Pet insurance

A little while ago, I wrote an article for a magazine about a little dog that was treated for tick paralysis. This dog was a spritely 12-year-old Jack Russell, the apple of his owners' eye and a fabulous pet for their two lively children. 'Buster' was happily romping at one of Sydney's Northern Beaches when was struck down by the tick. Within hours, Buster collapsed, labouring to breathe and distressed. His owners rushed him to us where we located and removed the tick and commenced treatment.

Buster's case turned out to be a complicated one, and he needed referral to a specialist where he spent several days in the ICU being ventilated and kept on intravenous fluids. It was touch-and-go on several occasions, but this dear family pet eventually pulled through.

The family are delighted to have their dog back, but he wasn't saved without a huge amount of work and a veterinary bill of almost $20,000.

When readers saw this figure, a number emailed in, asking for the typo to be corrected before thousands of pet owners get turned off vet treatment! Alas, this was no typing error. While such a large bill is unusual, with advances in technology, animals can now have almost any treatment available for humans. Most vet hospitals now do ultrasounds on a regular basis, many have digital X-Ray machines, perform chemotherapy routinely, do blood transfusions, repair cruciate ligaments, fractures and have in-house laboratory facilities. Specialist veterinary centres have even more impressive facilities. Many can do CT scans and some even have MRI facilities.

Without getting on the vet bandwagon, it's worth noting that, while the government pays for expensive human diagnostic equipment in public hospitals, vets mostly have to buy all their own equipment. This is where veterinary care becomes more expensive than human medical care—some of this equipment can run into the millions of dollars to purchase. The message here is that veterinary care is expensive and is only going to get more so with technologic advancements. The best way to safeguard yourself against these expenses is to have pet insurance. I have pet insurance for my own pets—of course, I treat most things myself, but if specialist referral became necessary, I feel safer knowing I will not have to foot the whole bill!

Pet insurance has been popular for years. When I practised in the UK 10 years ago, we spent at least an hour each day filling in claim forms for clients. It has taken a while for pet insurance to catch on in other countries, but it is becoming more and more popular, and from what I see at work, the insurance companies are all very reliable. If you are considering getting insurance, make sure you ring around and compare premiums and fine print.

IF YOUR DOG DOESN'T LIKE SOMEBODY, YOU PROBABLY SHOULDN'T EITHER.

ANON

Travel sickness

For the vast majority of dogs, travel sickness is more a result of anxiety and stress than actual motion sickness. The noise, sights, sounds and jolting movement dog's experience in a car is very foreign to what they encounter in their every day lives. Couple this with the fact that, right from puppyhood, car travel is often associated with an unpleasant outcome (being removed from their mother and litter mates, the first vet visit, etc) and it's no surprise our dogs can be apprehensive.

The best way to ensure you have a travel-friendly pet is to slowly acclimatize him to the car, and always to have a positive outcome at the end of the journey.

Start by having the dog sit in the car with you present. Don't go anywhere. It's not even necessary to close the door. Just have him in the car, get him to sit, and reward this.

Once the dog is happy enough in the car, practice restraining it. All dogs must be restrained inside the car, whether it be with a car harness (inexpensive harness that clips to the seat belt or in a crate in the back of the car). It is very dangerous to drive around with the dog running loose.

Always reward the dog for calm behaviour.

Next, take the dog on a very short, two to five-minute trip. Have a ball game or similar as a reward after this. Try to practice again and again, so that you are slowly desensitising the dog from the car travel, and always associate it with a positive outcome.

If the dog reacts badly, you will need to take a few steps backward and start again, gradually building up the journey time.

Don't make a fuss of your dog while it is whining and panicking—this only serves as it's proof that there must be something to worry about!

Once you can drive for 30 minutes without a problem, you're pretty much there.

Here are some more tips for making the journey more comfortable:
- Don't feed the dog for three to four hours before travel. They are less likely to vomit or have diarrhoea on an empty stomach.
- Make sure the dog goes to the toilet before you leave.
- Have the dog well restrained inside the car.
- Looking out the window can bring on nausea in dogs, so consider crate training and move the crate into the car for travel.
- Be careful when driving. Slow down and take bends carefully.
- Keep the car at a comfortable temperature.
- Avoid dehydration by having frequent water stops.

How to give a dog a tablet

Many clients get quite distressed about the thought of having to give a tablet to their pet. As with everything else, it's easier if you start giving tablets (even 'fake' ones) at a young age, but to tell the truth, medicating pets isn't difficult at all. You just need to be prepared to get your hands dirty!

First, with using the hand you don't write with, place your hand over the top of the pup's muzzle, and with your thumb and forefinger, fold the top lips into the mouth and around the teeth. This way, the pet cannot bite you.

Have the tablet between the pointer (1st) and tall (2nd) fingers of the writing hand.

Gently pull the dog's head back with the hand you have its muzzle gripped in, and it will automatically open its mouth. When the mouth opens, firmly hold the head right back and push the tablet into the mouth. You will need to push your fingers right into the mouth, near to the throat, in one decisive, quick movement. You are trying to get the tablet behind the tongue, where it will automatically be swallowed.

Don't worry about the dog biting you when you have your hands in its mouth. Usually It will gag to try and get your hand out, but biting in this situation is almost impossible.

- Use some gumption! One quick, strong and decisive movement is pain free for you and the pet. Dogs will give you one good chance, but most have no patience for incompetence.
- Lots of praise, and a treat (if it's allowed with the medication) is essential.

First aid for pets

There will likely be at least one situation in a pet owner's life when they need to apply some kind of first aid.

Two things you always need to remember are firstly that all animals, no

matter how friendly they may be at other times, will bite when they are in pain, and, in all first aid situations, contact your vet as soon as possible.

There are many different circumstances where first aid is needed. Below I have outlined a few and given the initial guidance.

What if a dog has been hit by a car?

Approach the dog calmly and carefully. Observe whether it is still breathing. Apply some kind of muzzle to protect yourself (such as winding a sock around the mouth or using a tie or belt). If the dog is not breathing, you can try to resuscitate by blowing into the nose once every five seconds or so. If you have a second person, they can massage the chest in between the blowing. Carefully move the dog off the road and into the vehicle you will be transporting it in. Use a blanket or a plank of wood if you have one. Contact the closest vet and transport the dog there as soon as possible.

How do I make a dog vomit?

Under some circumstances, such as if your pet has eaten a poison like snail bait, rat poison or chocolate, it is useful if you can make the dog vomit. Always check with the vet if this is appropriate. For some foreign body ingestions such as fish hooks with line attached, or large objects like pieces of tennis ball, making the dog vomit can have disastrous consequences.

The best thing to use to cause vomiting is washing soda crystals. Half a teaspoon of these on the back of the dog's tongue will generally cause it to vomit within a few minutes.

Always make sure:

1. You contact the vet and take the animal down as soon as possible—even with vomiting, dogs can absorb lethal amounts of some toxins.
2. You supervise the dog while it is vomiting to make sure it doesn't eat the vomit straight up again.

How do I stop bleeding?

If your dog has sustained a cut or gash, applying pressure is the best way to stop bleeding. Wrap a firm bandage around the area. For limbs, start at the foot and work upwards so you are not cutting off the circulation. If you have clipped a nail too short, dip the end into a soft cake of soap to try and 'plug' the vessel, and then bandage.

Things to have in a first aid kit

A small first aid kit is an excellent thing to have in the house and in the car in case of a pet emergency. Store it in a small plastic tub with a tight fitting lid and keep it in a safe (but easy to find) place.

Phone numbers:
- number and directions to the vet and an after hours vet nearby if applicable
- poison control centre

Equipment and supplies:
- a muzzle or roll of gauze to make a muzzle
- scissors
- tweezers.
- nylon lead
- cotton wool balls
- disposable gloves\
- towel or blanket to use as a stretcher

Bandage materials:
- square gauze
- rolls of bandage, both gauze and vet wrap types (these stick to themselves and don't adhere to the skin)
- band-aids (for humans)

Medicines:
- wound disinfectant such as betidine or chlorhexidine
- eye wash solution

- sterile saline solution for flushing wounds.
- activated charcoal to absorb ingested poison (check with the vet before administering).
- washing soda crystals to induce vomiting (again, check with vet).

4
MANNERS MAKETH THE PET

One of the most important things dog owners must concentrate on is obedience. If your dog does not obey commands, it becomes unruly. There's nothing worse than a delinquent dog let loose in the park, that attacks other dogs at whim, refuses to return to his owner and generally makes a nuisance of himself. Pretty soon, the downward spiral starts. Owners don't want to neglect the dog, but because they can't control it, it never goes out for a walk. Consequently, it barks all day out of boredom and decimates the garden. This is not the dog's fault you know, it's the owner's. Through a lack of training and understanding, they've inadvertently turned man's best friend into his biggest pest.

Behaviour and training issues are one of the most common cause of pet owners presenting their animal to the vet. These issues are also the biggest reason for surrender of pets to pounds and welfare shelters, and the largest cause of voluntary euthanasia of our animals. There are literally hundreds of commands your dog can learn and similarly, tens of different behavioural issues and problems they can have. In this chapter, I have outlined the most common ones I see in my hospital, and included a few of the perennially popular questions asked by my clients and the viewers of *Sunrise* and *The Morning Show*. For some of the obedience training information, I've enlisted the help of my friend and expert animal trainer, Vicki Austin, of Pet Resorts Australia.

Puppy parties

When puppies are as young as 10 weeks old, they can begin training at puppy parties. Most vets and pet shops will run these courses and aside from being great fun, they are also a valuable time for pups to socialize with other dogs and people and to learn the basic commands.

The best time for making your pet sociable with both people and other animals is during the 'imprinting' age. This is between 6 weeks and 14 weeks of age and is when your dog forms the social habits of a lifetime.

Puppy parties usually consists of a small group of, say 5 to 6 pups, and their owners as well as an animal trainer. The course is usually about an hour in length and you will progressively learn several basic commands. The classes concentrate on:

- Socialisation and 'manners' between dogs and with people
- Commands such as 'sit', 'stay' 'heel' and 'come'

You will also learn lots of other information on puppy health and nutrition.

Obedience classes

Most councils will have information on obedience classes held in your area. I would thoroughly recommend them for further socialization, training and good fun.

Sending your pet away to be trained

Some boarding kennels and training institutions offer a facility where you can have your pet trained intensively while it boards with them. For many people, while they want a well behaved and brilliantly trained pet, either they just cannot find enough time to do the whole thing themselves, or they are having trouble and need the dog to spend just a few weeks as a top up at 'boarding school'.

This can be an excellent adjunct to your own training, especially when you need somewhere to board your dog while you are on holidays. However, it is not fail-safe, especially if you've put Fido there because you are time poor. You need to have enough time at the 'hand back' for the trainer to explain exactly what commands have been taught, and how you should be using them. The dog will come back well trained, but if you're not, then the whole exercise will be pointless.

The basics: teaching your pup to 'sit' and 'stay'

Every dog needs to know how to sit, stay, heel and come when called. These are the basics and they allow you to communicate directly with your dog. The easiest commands are sit and stay.

'Sit' and 'stay'

As with any training, the secret is to be consistent and patient. You must always set the dog up for success (only ask it to sit for example, when it is in a position to sit, not when you know that sitting is impossible). Always make sure the dog sits when you ask it—if you start saying sit, then walk away when it ignores you, it will soon learn that sitting is optional.

Arm yourself with treats. While standing, reach down to near the puppy's level and hold a small treat just above the puppy's nose, moving it slowly backwards to between its ears. With the treat in this position, the puppy will naturally sit down. When it sits, praise the dog, say the command and give the treat. Don't hold the treat too high, because the puppy's natural instinct will then be to jump up. At first, you may have to gently press its bottom onto the ground. Say 'sit' as you do this, then lavish praise and reward.

Be enthusiastic—the more you vary your voice the better the dog will feel when it has done something good, then an upbeat, happy and enthusiastic voice reinforces your being pleased with it.

For the stay command, have the dog sitting first, then slowly walk backwards, saying 'stay'. Start by moving back a short distance only at first, gradually working towards a longer distance. Slowly move back and if the dog waits for you, give it a treat and once again, plenty of praise.

I find giving a hand signal (I usually hold up my palm) works well in conjunction. If you combine a hand signal with the verbal command for each different instruction, you can eventually ask the dog to sit or stay, for example, using hand signals only.

THE GREATEST PLEASURE OF A DOG IS THAT YOU MAY MAKE A FOOL OF YOURSELF, AND NOT ONLY WILL HE NOT SCOLD YOU, BUT HE WILL MAKE A FOOL OF HIMSELF TOO.
SAMUEL BUTLER

How to toilet train a puppy

Being a vet, you'd think my own dog would have been beautifully toilet trained from the very beginning, right? That's certainly what my husband and friends expected. But Minou, I'm ashamed to admit, was an absolute nightmare in that department. Far from the demure, impeccably groomed (well, maybe not all the time) image she portrays in her *Sunrise* and *Morning Show* gigs, my darling dog always preferred the carpet to the lawn (and absolutely refused to entertain the idea of weeing on the pavers of our courtyard—all the splashing was too much for her to bear).

Now that I am older and wiser and have the personal experience to match all the literature we studied at university, I have the toilet training business down to a fine art with Minou. I realize now that I left one very important step out of the process. I never restricted Minou's access to certain parts of the house, allowing her far too much of our house in which to find toileting locations. Crate training, explained elsewhere in the book, would have prevented Minou's toileting hiccups. The secret to toilet training is patience—remember the six Ps (pardon the pun!): *Persistence and patience prevent pesky peeing and pooing!*

Some background

When puppies are first born, they are unable to eliminate their own waste. The mother licks them to stimulate defecation and urination, and dutifully cleans up as she goes. By the time pups reach 3 weeks of age, they are able to urinate and defecate unassisted. They are usually not mobile enough to go outside the nest however, so the mother continues to keep the nesting area clean. As the puppies become more mobile, they will instinctively move away from the nest in order to toilet. Breeders assist this process by providing a different floor surface outside their bedding. They will instinctively search for an absorbent area to toilet—such as grass or carpet. As puppies continue to mature, they will move further and further from their nesting area. Like our own toddlers though, they will continue to have 'little accidents' throughout the toilet training process. Mum will continue to keep the nest clean and will not scold them for any mistakes. If we never interfered with the toileting habits of a puppy living in our home, and simply cleaned up without comment, the puppy's instincts would have him clean in your home by adulthood. However, due to a variety of influences (mostly human interference) many puppies' instincts in regard to toilet training become confused. Below is a fast track toilet training process suitable for all healthy puppies from 8 weeks of age.

- Limit access: A puppy cannot possibly understand that your entire home is the pack's nest and needs to be kept clean. Therefore while you are going through the toilet training stage, you will need to restrict the pups indoor access to certain areas of the home—this means crate training, conditioning the puppy to reside in small rooms such as the bathroom or laundry, or securing the pup on a lead. Failing this, you will need to give your pup your full and undivided attention. Take the pup out to toilet in your chosen toileting area every 30 minutes at first. If they oblige, give them a special treat or game that is reserved for this behaviour. Keep a container of treats at the location so you don't forget.

- Reward, don't reprimand: Your puppy is likely to have the occasional accident but you must be careful not to reprimand or show your disapproval in any way. By reprimanding you're causing confusion—your puppy will not understand that it shouldn't have eliminated, it will simply think it shouldn't eliminate in your presence. This will mean that next time you take it outside, it may not eliminate in the chosen spot, with you present, for fear of being disciplined! Furthermore, as soon as you let it back inside, it will rush through the house to find an appropriate, quiet spot away from the nest (usually the bedroom or the lounge room, where it can eliminate without you watching). See how everything can get so mixed up!

- Watch for the obvious times your pup will need to eliminate. These include after feeding, after a big drink, during a walk and after a big play session. Make sure you take him to 'the spot' at these times.

- Know your puppy's body language: Most pups will start to sniff, circle or whine before they urinate of defecate. When you get the signal, scoop the dog up and take it straight to the toilet location.

- Thoroughly clean up mistakes. Place any solid waste in the toileting area (this further reinforces that this is where the dog needs to go). Clean up urine using an enzymatic cleaner (such as 'urine off' spray, or you can use Biozet enzymatic washing powder or similar). The enzymatic cleaners break down the protein in the urine, eliminating the smell. NEVER use ammonium or chlorine based cleaners (such as bleach) to clean the area—to us it might smell clean but to dogs, the ammonia just smells like another dog's urine, and they will pee straight over the top of it!

- Make sure your puppy is kept clean at all times. If it has a soiled coat, it will see no reason to keep the living areas clean.
- If you feed the pup inside and keep the water bowl indoors as well, this may help to reinforce your pup's understanding that the house is the nest and must be kept clean.

Take the blame for any mistakes yourself. You simply were not paying enough attention. Reprimanding a puppy for a bodily function will only create anxiety. By reprimanding you will not make the puppy feel guilty for toileting—it will only learn that toileting in your presence is bad news!

When should we expect the pup to be toilet trained?
Most puppies will be largely toilet trained by 12 weeks of age, with just the occasional accident.

Crate training
Crate training can be an efficient and effective way to house train a dog. Dogs do not like to soil their resting/sleeping quarters if given adequate opportunity to eliminate elsewhere. Temporarily confining your dog to a small area strongly inhibits the tendency to urinate and defecate. However, there is still a far more important aspect of crate training.

If your dog does not eliminate while she is confined, then she will need to eliminate when she is released, i.e. she eliminates when you are present to reward and praise her.

Be sure to understand the difference between temporarily confining your dog to a crate and long-term confinement when you are not home. The major purpose of confinement when you are not home is to restrict mistakes to a small protected area. The purpose of crate training is quite the opposite. Short-term confinement to a crate is intended to inhibit your dog from eliminating when confined, so that she will want to eliminate when released from confinement and taken to an appropriate area. Crate training also helps teach your dog to have bladder and bowel control. Instead of going whenever she feels like it, she learns to hold it and go at convenient scheduled times.

Crate training should not be abused, otherwise the problem will get drastically worse. The crate is not intended as a place to lock up the dog and forget her for extended periods of time. If your dog soils her crate because you left her there too long, the house training process will be set back several weeks, if not months.

Your dog should only be confined to a crate when you are at home. Except at night, give your dog an opportunity to relieve herself every hour. Each time you let her out, put her on leash and immediately take her outside. Once outside, give her about three to five minutes to produce. If she does not eliminate within the allotted time period, simply return her to her crate. If she does perform, then immediately reward her with praise, food treats, affection, play, an extended walk and permission to run around and play in your house for a couple of hours. For young pups, after 45 minutes to an hour, take her to her toilet area again. *Never give your dog free run of your home unless you know without a doubt that her bowels and bladder are empty.*

During this crate training procedure, keep a diary of when your dog eliminates. If you have her on a regular feeding schedule, she should soon adopt a corresponding elimination schedule. Once you know what time of day she usually needs to eliminate, you can begin taking her out only at those times instead of every hour. After she has eliminated, she can have free, but supervised, run of your house. About one hour before she needs to eliminate (as calculated by your diary) put her in her crate. This will prevent her from going earlier than you had planned. With your consistency and abundance of rewards and praise for eliminating outside, she will become more reliable about holding it until you take her out. Then the amount of time you confine her before her scheduled outing can be reduced, then eliminated.

> ## DO NOT MAKE THE MISTAKE OF TREATING YOUR DOGS LIKE HUMANS, OR THEY WILL TREAT YOU LIKE DOGS.
>
> MARTIN SCOTT

Separation anxiety

Separation anxiety is the inability of a dog to cope in the absence of its owner. Sometimes dogs are breed predisposed (Cavalier King Charles spaniels and Staffordshire Bull Terriers are good examples) but it is usually a result of owners not being diligent in teaching the new puppy to spend time on its own. It is made worse in situations where puppies are not adequately trained, exercised or socialized with other dogs or people.

Let me start here by telling you a little story about a puppy called 'Fifi'. I first met Fifi on a busy Monday morning, when she and her owner burst through the doors of the surgery waiting room needing to speak to a vet immediately. No real emergency. The owner just needed some urgent advice on what she should do with the dog for 'show and tell' at her son's school where she was headed presently. There was little Fifi, clutched tightly to her owners chest, draped in a brand new swarovski crystal collar and sporting the latest in chic canine couture jackets. Fifi's mummy is very nervous about introducing her to 25 active 7-year-olds, especially since little Fifi rarely leaves the house (the owner feels the pup prefers to watch TV with her than go to the park and didn't want to force the issue). Fifi also prefers to spend the afternoon with mum when her boys have friends to visit. As a vet, little alarm bells start going off all over the place in this situation—anxious, overprotective owners with child substitute puppies usually result in adult dogs with separation anxiety—what we in the business call the 'velcro dog syndrome'.

I needed to give this new dog owner plenty of valuable advice—and not just about how to manage a 'show and tell' experience! But there is only so much that can be done in three minutes. In desperation, I bundled her off with her spare arm full of pamphlets on puppy socialisation classes, training hints and everything else I could think of. Predictably, Fifi returned to the clinic about 12 months later. This little bundle of joy has now developed into a furball of terror. Fifi cannot stand to be alone for even one minute. She sleeps in bed with the owner because if she is left in the laundry, she yelps and squeals all night. The husband is now relegated to the spare room in order to get some sleep (the once tiny Labrador Retriever puppy now takes up a substantial amount of room in the bed).

Fifi's owner has started a morning exercise program and now needs to spend several hours in the morning away from the house. The dog starts to panic about the family leaving the minute the alarm clock goes off in the morning. It follows the family around, jumps up when it hears the keys rattle, rams at the back door and spends the whole time it is alone yelping, barking and tearing up the garden. The family thought that starting a morning walk routine might help, but Fifi has no idea of lead etiquette—she pulls on the lead so hard she almost knocks her owner over. She also hates all other dogs and has no social skills with children either.

After a series of huge bills for repair of furniture and a complete garden overhaul, and numerous complaints and threats by the neighbours and the council, the owners are desperate. They want out. This story may sound extreme, but believe me, vets all around the world see this situation every week. It all stems from the way you bring the puppy up.

Golden rules for curing a 'velcro dog'

Every puppy must learn to spend time alone. This should be for at least two hours a day. Crate training is very useful for this.

1. All puppies must be taught to sit, stay, and relax, and be rewarded for this. This is where most owners go wrong—they want to expose the dog to departures before they have taught the dog an alternative response to panic. You will need to teach the dog to stay on its mat, in a relaxed state for progressively longer periods of time (up to 30 minutes) by continually reminding it to sit and stay, and rewarding the relaxed behaviour.

2. Teach the dog that attention seeking behaviour (jumping, barking) does not get attention—they must be ignored (talking or acknowledging this behaviour at all, even to reprimand, is considered a reward for a desperate dog). On the other hand, when the dog is lying quietly anywhere, it should always be rewarded.

3. All the departure cues that trigger the anxiety response need to be decoupled from the actual departure. You may have to pick up the keys or lock the doors many times a day without actually leaving.

4. Sometimes ignoring the dog for a good 20 minutes prior to leaving and after coming home works well to prevent the dog getting 'worked up'. If this is not possible, then make sure you act calmly around the dog before leaving it. All that frantic cuddling and kissing as well as the declarations of undying love and promises of a speedy return (always said using a high pitched, frantic voice tone) will only get the dog over excited and highly anxious.

5. Medications are sometimes necessary, especially at the start of treatment. Some dogs are in such a high anxiety state that they are unable to be calm for long enough to learn any basic commands, let alone be calm on a mat for a period of time. These medicines are usually anti-depressants or anxiolytics and are used to calm the dog enough so the training can actually take place.

Teaching a dog to come when called

One of the most common training problems faced by dog owners is lack of controllability on walks. Many pet owners report that their pup starts off well, but later on, will only return when called if there is nothing better on offer. There are three main reasons why your dog may suddenly fail to take notice:

1. Your dog may be highly motivated to do something else—follow a scent, play with another animal or chase something. This is probably the most common problem.

2. Sometimes it might be that the dog hasn't been properly trained to come when called and if fact, inadvertently trained not to obey the 'come' command! Some owners will make the mistake of scolding the dog when it finally does come, but later than desired. Owners interpret the dogs response (usually they approach with their head and tail held down, avoiding eye contact), as the dog feeling guilty. You'll hear them say 'He knows he's done something wrong'. This is far from the case. The dog is simply being submissive, and knows from past experience that it is punished when it comes so, understandably enough, it starts to avoid coming for as long as possible.

3. The third reason a dog may not come when it is called has to do with dominance. Some dogs that ignore commands usually also have dominance/aggression symptoms. Does your dog growl when you take its bone away, order it to do something, or brush or bathe it? Is your dog generally disobedient, stubborn, pushy and slow to obey? This is a dominance-related problem. Later in the chapter there are hints on how to handle these pups.

THE DOG WAS CREATED SPECIALLY FOR CHILDREN. HE IS THE GOD OF FROLIC.
HENRY WARD BEECHER.

Training your dog to come when called on walks

- Start early. Up until the puppy is 12 weeks of age, it will automatically want to keep close to the pack for protection. If you train at this age, you will be taking advantage of the fact that the puppy wants to come to you anyway.

- Take an ample supply of tasty treats with you on the walk, and always reward the puppy for the recall command. Don't use the reward at any other time.

- Be consistent. As the puppy gets older, it will gain confidence and will discover there are other options to coming when called. Don't allow the puppy to ignore the command at any time. If you do, you are teaching the dog that the command is optional.

- Start by having the puppy on a lead. Walk backwards away from the dog, still loosely holding the lead, away. Hold out the food treat and when the dog follows, say the command 'come' in a happy, animated tone of voice. Lavish praise on the pup for coming when it has been called and immediately give the treat. Start to move backwards more quickly, say the command 'come'. Stop and move the treat reward above the dog's head to bring him into a 'sit' position. Teaching the dog to 'sit' before the recall command will make this step much easier. Praise the dog and keep rewarding it while it is in the sitting position. Then give the release command, something like 'okay'.

- The lead is essential at first because it gives you the opportunity to block any incorrect response. With the lead you can block any attempt by the dog to ignore the command—such as sniffing the ground or moving towards some other distraction. The next step is to have someone else hold the dog on the lead, standing about 5 to 10m away from you. The person should release the lead when you give the command 'come'. The dog will come to you for the treat and sit.

There are four golden rules that help to make this training successful:

1. *Never punish the dog for not coming quickly enough.* As I explained at the beginning, this only trains the dog to delay obeying the command for as long as possible.

2. *Always have the reward ready.* Start to vary the reward (different food treats, a ball, chewy toy etc) and make it a surprise each time. The dog will always return, wondering if this time it has hit the 'jackpot', whatever its favourite reward may be.

3. *Set the dog up for success.* Use the lead initially, then always make sure you issue the command when the dog is going to obey, for example, in the training phase, don't issue the 'come' command while the dog is running with other dogs or is otherwise distracted

4. *Don't put the lead on the dog as soon as it has returned, even if it is time to go home.* The dog will then associate coming back with going home. First, give it the treat, lavish praise and play a few other training games. Then put the lead on after a time, giving further praise.

Correcting destructive behaviour in puppies

Biting and chewing up small objects is a completely normal behaviour of puppies. The trouble is, we don't like it so we need to try and change their instinctive behaviour so it fits with our household. Here are the training methods I find most helpful in correcting these problems:

1. Stopping chewing furniture and other objects

When the dog isn't supervised, make sure you have it confined to a 'puppy proof' area or in a blocked off area of a room, or even in a large crate, where it has access to things it is allowed to chew. This sounds very hard, I know, because we all want our little buddy to have free roam but this initial stage is very important, both for toilet training and for preventing lifetime habits of chewing furniture and other objects.

Have a variety of toys, raw hides and nylon bones for the dog to chew on. Don't give him any items of human interest such as an old slipper, this will only reinforce his tendency to hunt down shoes of any type throughout the house.

Encourage the puppy to chew the appropriate objects. You can do this by giving the dog the objects often, or using them to play games of tug of war or similar.

Try to divert the dog's attention away from inappropriate objects to its toys *before* it starts chewing on them. If you direct it to another toy and play with it after it has started chewing, for example, furniture, it will perceive this as a reward for chewing the furniture.

If you catch the dog in the act, it can be reprimanded with a firm 'NO'. This does not work unless the dog is just about to chew, or is chewing the object.

Unacceptable objects can be booby trapped, such as laced with pepper. The advantage of this is that punishment in this case is immediate.

2. Stopping biting during play

Normal play behaviour of puppies can be very aggressive. In the litter, puppies are constantly tussling, usually biting each other around the head and neck area. When they leave the confines of their litter, we become their playmates and they will, naturally, attempt to play with us in the same way. This has to be changed, not only because puppies have needle sharp teeth, but also because if this play behaviour continues into adulthood, they might inadvertently cause damage to someone.

Unfortunately, when most of us encounter an aggressively playful puppy, who, for example, starts biting at our ankles, jumping up to nip at hands or tugging at trousers, we become flustered (or in the case of children and the elderly, quite scared) and our reaction is to push the dog away, or smack it. For the dog, this merely signals that 'you're up for a game' and its behaviour will intensify.

Possible causes of playful aggression

1. Genetic predisposition. Some breeds are more highly motivated to play. For example Jack Russel Terriers and Staffodshire Bull Terriers.
2. Unintentional owner initiation of aggressive play, for example, playing aggressive games such as tug of war, chasing and fighting.
3. Stimulation by the victim. For example, trying to hit the dog, pulling away or chasing the dog will only intensify its behaviour.
4. Lack of obedience training. It's hard to tell a dog to stop something if it doesn't know basic commands.
5. Unintentional reinforcement of the behaviour. This will happen when you play with the dog in response to its aggressive solicitation of the play.
6. Lack of owner dominance. Some dogs are disobedient/hard to control because they are dominant over their owner.
7. Inadequate care and maintenance of the dog. Lack of opportunity to play with other dogs and poor socialisation.

Treating playful aggression in puppies

- Avoid physical punishment, but let the dog know it has hurt you by either squealing or yelping, then stop the play immediately. Walk away and give the dog a chance to calm down.
- For dogs that do not calm down, use the 'time out' method. Send the dog to the laundry or put it outside for a time. At first, the time out should be done for a very short amount of time, say, 10 seconds. The next time, increase the time out—go to, say 20 seconds and so on.
- An alternative to the time out method is the **control method**. For this method, you will need to put the puppy in the control position (also called the heel position).
- **The heel position is when the puppy is sitting on the owners**

left side, facing the same direction. Take the lead in the right hand, short down near the clip, or by pushing two of your right fingers through the puppy's collar. Your left hand remains free to swing the puppy's bottom into the correct sitting position. This way you have control of the puppy at both ends—he no longer has choices. The very moment the puppy's bottom arrives in the correct position ,the tension MUST be taken out of the lead and the grip OFF the collar. The puppy will probably try to charge away at this time. You must then pull the puppy back into line and into the heel position. The idea is for the puppy to sit in the heel position without straining or pulling, and therefore to give control over to the owner. *The puppy will only regain his freedom when he has given up any fighting, and handed over control to you, for at least 10 seconds.*

- Avoid any games involving tests of strength, such as tug of war play fighting or chasing.
- Avoid unintentionally rewarding the dog by throwing it a treat or toy to distract it.
- Encourage more appropriate, non-aggressive games such as ball or frisbee chasing.
- Take the dog at least twice a day to a place where it can play with and socialize with other dogs.
- Never leave a child alone with a dog. This applies at any time. Even though this might be play behaviour, for a child this can be extremely frightening, and potentially serious as facial injuries may result.

Begging and pestering for food or attention

Since food and attention are the two things most dogs crave in life, it's no surprise they will go to any lengths to get it. Most dogs will try begging at the dinner table for scraps, jumping up, pushing owners, whining and barking for attention or food. Some dogs even have bizarre behaviours they employ to get what they want. I had a patient that needed several weeks with its leg in a cast to repair a fracture. During this time, it must have had more treats and attention than ever before in its life (understandably) because once the cast was removed, it developed a 'sympathy lameness' where it would intermittently limp on one of its legs, in a bid for attention (all medical follow ups were done and clear). This is an uncommon, but well documented problem.

When she first started training, my own dog, Minou, would sometimes follow me around and excitedly sit, drop, roll over and play dead over and over again to try and get that extra reward.

Stopping that behaviour can be hard for us pet owners, because often we see it as cute, or even funny. It soon gets pretty annoying having a dog bark continuously while the family is eating, or jumping up at you (or your guests) to try and remove food from your hand. The earlier you start to deal with the problem, the easier it will be to solve.

The rules

1. Make it a hard and fast family rule that the dog is NEVER rewarded for begging and pestering. No exceptions. The dog must be ignored when it starts the behaviour, until it stops—even if this takes several minutes.

2. If the dog is becoming so unruly that it is impossible to ignore, then either get up and leave the room, or scold it (just shout firmly, don't terrify or belt it) enough to stop the behaviour immediately.

3. Expect the dog to get worse as you ignore its pleas for the first few days. Don't give up—if you stick with the program, you WILL win the battle.

4. Be consistent. Make sure the whole family is consistent too.

Aggression in dogs

Aggression problems in dogs make up a great deal of the case load of veterinary behavioural specialists. There are many different types and causes of aggression. In this book, I have provided a brief outline. If your pet has an aggression problem, do not delay in seeking advice from your vet. Most of these cases can be solved with early, professional intervention.

It is worth noting that much of the behaviour we see as aggressive, is just fairly natural for a dog. In the wild, wolves and feral dogs run in packs. These packs generally consist of dogs that are related to each other and the group stay close together within a certain territory. The pack hunts for food, and guards its territory. The relationship between one pack and a neighbouring one is usually quite antagonistic. Two neighbouring packs will often attack each other in competition for mates, food and territory. Within packs there will be struggles from time to time as well. A dominant male may be challenged by another to become a pack leader.

In contrast with its wild days, the modern dog finds itself in an environment which it would hardly recognize—humans do not have a territory which they defend. Strangers come to the house and are greeted rather than being attacked, they go about their business, and leave again, with only an initial suspicious glance from the dog. On their daily walks, dogs and owners move through a sea of indifferent strangers and friendly acquaintances. They meet strange dogs of all shapes and sizes, one or two known enemies waiting for the daily face off, and a few perpetual juveniles, always happy to have a romp and a play.

The wild dog's world is a much simpler place than the one we have created and put them in. It's no surprise that from time to time, the wires get crossed, and dogs react in a more primitive, sometimes more aggressive way than we had imagined.

Here are the major types of aggression displayed by dogs:

1. *Dominance aggression.* This type of aggression is usually directed towards family members and often in response to a dominant gesture from the owner, such as petting, scolding or grooming. It can also be displayed in competitive situations such as competition over a resting place or food. With dominance aggression situations, an owner will often comment that a dog is 'moody' and reacts 'unprovoked'. With this type of aggression, the dog is often not aggressive to all family members, but only certain ones. It is usually non aggressive with strangers—the problem is not to do with the strangers, only the family member. It tends to be the type of dog that exhibits other dominance postures over the owner when it is not aggressive—such as staring or jumping up at them. With dominance aggression, the dog is often reported as being 'not himself', getting a strange look in his eyes and ears standing erect, as well as the fur erect along the back. After the attack, these dogs will usually go back to being very friendly. These dogs often enforce arbitrary and sometimes bizarre 'rules' governing how family members may behave. One dog would not let a certain member of the family into the swimming pool while others were in it, and another client reported that her German Shepherd would not let her daughter sit on the couch in the television room. These dogs are like night and day. Vicious, then affectionate, all in one transaction. This type of aggression is often the most dangerous and needs careful veterinary treatment. There are many causes and management solutions which go far beyond the scope of this book.

2. *Defensive aggression towards family members.* This is when the dog reacts to what it considers to be a threat to its health and wellbeing. Examples of this are a dog lashing out at an owner when they are pulling its hair, medicating it, hitting or otherwise hurting the dog.

In this situation, owners unwittingly reward the dog in many cases by stopping the offending procedure when the dog lashes out.

3. *Fear aggression.* This type of aggression is a self-protective aggression when the dog is aggressive towards the animal or person it is afraid of, and trying to escape. Quite often, the dog will wag its tail and look friendly; it may even, in fact, approach the person/dog it is afraid of, but will snap and bite immediately if a hand comes out to pat it. This is the most common type of aggression vets become a victim of. You should never punish fear aggression. Instead, the process of systematic counter conditioning and desensitisation works best, ie., repeatedly expose the dog, for a short time only, to the thing it is afraid of, and reward it for being calm in their company. Ignore the anxious behaviour. In a home situation, have the person the dog is fearful of take over feeding duties. Muzzles and tranquilizers sometimes need to be used.

Rather than analyze each individiual type of aggression, I have included the most common questions and concerns I hear in practice.

Q: We recently had a very bad experience with our pet dog that had to be euthanased because he was aggressive towards friends and also our children. We would like another dog, but can a test be done at an early age to guarantee the dog won't be aggressive?

Aggression towards people, particularly familiar people and owners, is the most common reason dogs are presented to animal behavioural specialists. We usually call this type of aggression dominance related.

The surprising thing for many owners is to learn that canine aggression is almost always normal behaviour. It might seem puzzling to the average pet owner that a dog would bite a member of its own family, but dogs are social animals, and they communicate using a wide repertoire of ritualized behaviours, aggression being one of these.

High risk situations for aggression of this type include:

- When a dog is protecting its possessions, such as food, stolen objects, treats or toys.
- When a dog is approached or spoken to while in its 'den'.(which could be in its kennel, under a table, chair or bed)
- When a favourite family member is approached or touched by another family member.
- When the dog feels that certain actions are a threat to its social standing in the household (this can include punishment by certain family members, as well as vocalising and petting).

Whether a certain dog is likely to bite is dependant on many things including genetics, age, sex and neurobiology. Most dogs will start to show aggression between the ages of one to three years. This coincides with sexual and social maturity. If your dog suddenly becomes aggressive older than, say at five or six, you should investigate any recent environmental causes, such as a new baby crying, death of a spouse etc.

Aggression is more common in male dogs. As for breed, there have been many different studies done with varying results. It is important to research the breeds you are thinking of quite thoroughly, being realistic about the environment the dog will find itself in. Breeders are usually very helpful in this area and you should discuss with them in detail the temperament their dogs have and how suitable it will be to your lifestyle.

There are many different temperament testing techniques that have been developed for puppies. These tests are performed when the puppy is quite young, around 7 weeks of age and involve scoring each individual on how readily it comes to the tester, if it will follow happily, how it responds to being restrained, petted on the head and back, and being lifted. These tests are much more accurate in mature animals as a predictor of temperament than they are in pups, and this is because dominance aggression usually doesn't set in until the dog reaches maturity.

As well as researching the breed and temperament testing, it is vital that any pet dog be well socialized and trained using a non-aggressive, positive reinforcement training technique. Puppy classes are available at most vet hospitals and training facilities and these serve to help pups develop social personalities towards other dogs and humans during that important imprinting age. Training, reinforcing and rewarding calm behaviour, teaching children as well as adults the correct ways to approach and interact with their dog should be done for every single new dog in our lives. This is our best guarantee of a well-mannered, happy and reliable pet.

Q: A dog broke off its chain and attacked a friend's dog as we were going for a walk. The dog had her by the neck and wouldn't let go. My wife was kicking the dog to try and get it off, but this wasn't working. The owner came over and pried the dog off by forcing her hand into the dog's mouth. Our dog ended up with cuts on her neck and ear. 1. What do you do if a larger dog is attacking your own dog? 2. What is the best way to subdue a dog if it is attacking something?

This is a very serious situation. On the one hand, breaking up any dog fight puts you at risk of being harmed. On the other, a dog's life may be at stake—or it could have been a child being attacked. Whatever you do, you should never, ever go to the front end of the animal. Never grab the dog by the scruff of its neck and do not put your hand in the dog's mouth.

Try to stay as calm as possible in this situation. Screaming, yelling, thumping and hitting the dog will only arouse the dog more and make matters worse.

Respected animal trainer Steve Austin recommends picking the dogs back legs up by the hocks, one in each hand and pulling the dog away, walking backwards. Steve says in 99 per cent of cases this will result in the dog letting go. In most cases, the dog will then walk away. You should then remove yourself from the scene, walking, not running, quietly away while keeping an eye on the dog. Do not let the victim run away either, as the dog is likely to chase it. If you can put some object, like a suitcase or chair, between you and the dog, that it a good idea.

The most important thing is to prevent this scenario from happening in the first place. While we are essentially a pet friendly world, all dogs, large or small, can bite, and any dog has the ability to inflict injury. Invariably, dogs involved in fights are inadequately trained, inadequately restrained and/or surrounded by (albeit well-meaning) people who have a lack of understanding of dog behaviour.

The best pets are a result of careful research prior to purchase, buying from respected breeders, attending puppy socialisation classes from an early age followed by at least basic training school. As well as this, children and adults in the family should be well educated about their pet.

Most dogs bite each other and people, because neither adults nor children have been educated about appropriate behaviour around dogs.

The animal protection societies worldwide have developed and implemented a ground breaking pet education programs are being introduced to schools. The programs are having great success, so if your school doesn't have it, approach them and suggest they look into it.

What to do if you are frightened by a dog

- Stand still like a statue.
- Clench your hands into fists and tuck them under your chin.
- If the dog knocks you over, roll into a tight ball putting your hands over your head and stay quiet and still. The dog will very likely get bored and go away.

Dogs and thunderstorms

Our dog's world is much different from ours. Their sense of smell is a thousand times better than our own (they can smell something we have cleaned off the floor six weeks ago!) and their hearing is far more acute. It's not surprising then, that dogs seem to pick up on impending weather changes and thunderstorms well before we do.

Dogs detect the changes in electrostatic charges of the atmosphere and barometric pressure changes as well as detecting low frequency noises. To a dog, a thunderstorm represents a mini environmental disaster, several hours before we even know it's on its way!

Owners of pooches with a thunderstorm phobia often have tales of their pets' frantic behaviour. Gardens are dug up, furniture overturned and some dogs will defecate and urinate in the house and over the furniture. Some will even jump through plate glass windows in order to escape.

Fireworks can cause a similar stress response in many dogs. I was once called out to an emergency during the New Year's Eve fireworks on Sydney Harbour. The owners of the dog had gone out to enjoy the celebrations, leaving the dog safely (or so they thought) inside their third storey unit, located near the waterfront. Unfortunately, as the fireworks display started, the terrified dog smashed through the lounge room window in a desperate attempt to escape the noise, landing three storeys below. His experience didn't end there—the poor thing then staggered onto the road, only to be hit by a car. The dog survived, but the owners returned home to find the new year had brought them a demolished home interior and a very sick little dog needing several thousand dollars worth of surgery.

The cause of thunderstorm anxiety and noise phobia may be both hereditary and learnt behaviour. Most commonly affected breeds include the herding dogs such as German Shepherds and Collies, the hounds such as Beagles and Bassets, as well as Labradors and Golden

Retrievers. Herding dogs are bred to be highly reactive and also to hide fear. This mix is likely to result in high anxiety.

These dogs can be helped to overcome their fear using a training process called systemic desensitisation and counter-conditioning. Basically, this involves exposing the dog to gradual increases in loudness of the thunderstorm noise using a tape recording and rewarding the dog for being relaxed when it is played.

Even if the dog gets upset well before the storm can be heard by people, it is still worthwhile desensitising him to the noise. It is likely that the dog will be less upset when the storm is overhead, and therefore may not react as badly when he knows it is approaching.

Desensitisation tapes and CDs can be purchased from your local vet. Tapes need to be played very softly at first, rewarding the dog for not reacting. Gradually increase the loudness and reward for relaxed behaviour each time. If the dog reacts, it means the noise has become too loud too quickly and you will have to go back a few steps. It is wise to have veterinary guidance for this program.

There are some other things you can do to help your dog. Try to make sure your dog always has a place to go for shelter. Animals dig and become destructive because they are searching for a safe place, and a good kennel, or den with some soundproofing will help.

Never baby talk to your dog through a storm. This is just a signal to him that the fear is okay. Don't try to calm him by giving him treats while he is fretting—this also teaches him that the reaction is good, and will be rewarded.

Interestingly, the most recent studies indicate that dogs with another dog in the household tend to manage their fear of storms better than single dogs do, even though the unaffected dog completely ignored the anxious dog during the storm. If you're game, you could get your frightened friend a pal.

A pheromone diffuser called DAP (dog appeasing pheromone) may also be helpful. This product contains a substance released by the lactating female dog that functions to calm puppies in times of stress. It has been found to successfully calm dogs in stressful environments and unpredictable situations. Pescriptions are available through vets.

Sometimes it will be necessary to tranquilize the dog during the first few training sessions. Various drugs are available and your vet will prescribe them, if needed, depending on whether the dog is better suited to sedation or anti-anxiety medication.

Preparing your pet for the arrival of a new baby

If you had a much loved pet and 'only child' before the arrival of your first human baby, what I'm going to tell you next will definitely ring bells. I've been through it myself and had it not been for my veterinary knowledge our trusty dog and 'only daughter' would have fared much worse. Remember them? That gorgeous dog whom you both spent hours crooning over. Who slept on your bed, ate only the best pet foods (sometimes even the best human foods) went on long, luxurious walks with you every day, accompanied you both on weekends away, played endlessly in the park, at the beach and went to dinner with you at friends' houses. That precious pet who only had to sneeze and you rushed him off to the vet like a worried parent?

They were always the perfectly behaved pets, but now that you have a new baby, things are just not the same. Fido seems to suddenly hate being outside, he's digging holes in the back garden, chewing his paws, barking endlessly and getting complaints from the neighbours.

This is a scenario that is quite often presented to vets. If you're expecting a new bub, or have a young baby, here are some tips that will make the transition for your pet (and you) much easier.

- *Make any adjustments to your pets lifestyle well in advance*. It is inevitable that you won't have as much time to walk the dog or pat the cat when the baby comes home, so during the months before the birth, gradually decrease the amount of time you spend with your pets. Sudden changes are not well tolerated and usually result in anxiety related behaviour problems.

- *Familiarise your pet with baby sounds and smells.* A baby's cry can be terrifying to a pet at first. Introduce your friend's baby to your dog. Buy (or make) a tape of a baby crying. Show your pet the new baby's room and once the baby is born, have someone take a blanket of the bub's home so the dog can get familiar with its new family member's scent. If your pet shows any anxiety as a result of these exposures, then more formal reward-based training should be repeated until the pet exhibits no problems in the presence of the stimuli.

- *If your pet is going to live outside once the baby is born, organize its new accommodation well in advance* so it is quite settled months earlier. If the pet will remain inside, think about ways to keep them out of the baby's room. Some people find erecting a screen door at the entrance to the nursery allows them to hear and see the baby but keeps unwanted guests out.

- *If there is no one available to walk the dog at all, think about getting a dog walker to visit two or three times a week.* This is essential as it stops them from becoming bored (which leads to barking, digging holes and general pesky behaviour).

- *For dogs, a review or upgrade of training skills is essential so that you can effectively control your dog in all situations.* This will be especially important as the baby grows and starts moving around. Practice each command in different rooms of the house, concentrate on commands that are least successful at the moment and use lots of rewards and praise. Any existing behaviour problems need to be resolved before the arrival of a baby.

And when the baby arrives...

The most important aspect of retraining your pet to accept a new baby is to reward it for being relaxed and obedient in the presence of a child.

Many pets soon learn that the presence of a baby is a time for inattention, confinement and even 'punishment' while the absence of the baby is a cue for 'good' things to happen.

This must be reversed:

- Make every effort to allow the pet into the room for food, play or affection when the baby is present.
- Feed the pet when the baby is being fed, or have another family member play with or do some reward training with the pet (sit, stay etc) when the baby is in the room.
- Take the dog outdoors for play or for a walk when you take the child out.

The goal is to teach the pet that positives or 'good things' are most likely to happen in the presence of the child.

What if your pet becomes aggressive towards children?

This behaviour is very upsetting for the whole family and thankfully not common, particularly if the pet has been well prepared for baby's arrival.

There are many different types of aggression including fear, predatory or territorial that tend to cause aggression as soon as the baby enters the your home, or possessive, play, or dominance aggression that may cause the dog to turn on the baby as he or she starts to get older and move around more.

You need to take immediate action if this situation arises. Make a realistic decision whether to keep the pet and work with it, or remove it from the house.

A visit to the vet is essential—they may recommend you see a veterinary behavioural specialist who can assess your pet and tell you what the chances are of a safe and effective treatment for your pet's aggression.

In the meantime, you must keep any aggressive dog or cat well restrained and away from any small children.

5
GROOMING AND NUTRITION

All time best grooming tips

Grooming your pet can be a pleasure, or a prize pain in the neck, depending on how you plan for it. If your dog heads for the door the minute it sees a shampoo bottle, I have a few tips that might make the process a bit easier.

- **Start early.** If you introduce your pup to the brush and bathtub at an early age, it will be much easier to handle. As well as this, practise getting your pet used to having its ears, face and feet cleaned. Even when you're not bathing him, examine his ears and toes regularly and also open his mouth to look at his teeth. Praise him lavishly and give him a reward for behaving while you do this.

- **Brush your dog before you bath him.** Getting the knots out first makes the coat much less likely to matt.

- **While you're brushing, use this opportunity to check for fleas.** Sprinkle the hairs and dander as well as some of the dirt from the coat onto a white piece of paper. Place a few drops of water on the black spots especially and wait a few minutes. If the water turns red, this means the dirt is dried blood, from flea droppings.

- **If you need to cut knots out, never cut across, parallel to the**

skin. This way you run the risk of cutting the skin. Put one blade of the scissor through the knot, facing away from the skin and perpendicular to it, then close the scissors to 'splice' the knot.

- **Always use warm water to bathe your pet and try to avoid spraying him with the hose—use a tub, or sponge him down instead.** A good strong hose down with freezing water is likely to turn even the most stoic of dogs off his bath session.
- **Always use a soap free, gentle shampoo and conditioner that is formulated for animal skin.** Never use human shampoos. A dog's skin is about 6 times thinner than ours and more sensitive. Steer clear of disinfecting products like eucalyptus and tea tree oil. These are very drying, and after all, we are only trying to clean our pets, not disinfect them!
- **Don't use wool wash.** The coat of some breeds might be wool, but the skin is a living organism. Use the appropriate products.
- **Brush the coat while you dry it.** This way knots come out much easier.
- **Never use a hot hair dryer.** If you use a hair dryer always have it on the cool setting, Heating the skin up too much can cause bacterial infections called hot spots.
- **If you use clipper blades, check them every few minutes to make sure they are cool.** They heat up very quickly and can cause nasty burns.
- **Make sure you get the coat completely dry.** Leaving the dog in the sun to dry out slowly can cause yeast and bacteria to flourish, resulting in infections.

Cleaning ears

Some dogs with long, pendulous ear flaps and those with long or narrowed ear canals can be prone to getting dirty and infected ears.

The best way to clean ears is just to get a ball of cotton wool, and scoop any muck away. I do not recommend using commercial ear cleaning solutions unless you have been specifically told to do so by your vet.

Many of these solutions are irritant and have no anti-bacterial agent in them and because of this, they often serve to moisten the ear canal even more, providing a nice place for bacteria and yeasts to grow—a warm, bacterial soup, if you like.

If you are getting a large amount of black, smelly or greasy discharge, you need to get the vet to check whether there is an infection present.

Cleaning eyes

Most of the time, eyes should be self cleaning. If there is any unusual discharge, see your vet to make sure your dog hasn't got conjunctivitis, a foreign body stuck in the eye, or an ulcer etc. Some dogs, due to their anatomy, have a mild eye discharge all the time, and the white breeds such as Maltese and Bichon Frise can have brown, tear staining marks extending down their cheeks.

While there are acid products that will bleach the staining, I don't recommend them. Like many vets, I have seen sore and damaged eyes as a result of improper use of these products. The best way to clean eyes is by gently bathing with a saline solution (not a teaspoon of salt in a cup of water, but saline for eyes which you can purchase from most chemists).

Cleaning teeth

There is a prevailing myth going around that it's okay and even perfectly natural for dogs to have putrid 'doggy breath'. *Let me make it clear that a dog's breath should not smell*. If there is a foul odour, it is a sign that there is something wrong.

Dogs are prone to getting deposits of plaque and tartar on their teeth. The tartar harbours bacteria that start to cause inflammation and redness of the gums (gingivitis) The halitosis (bad breath) is caused from by-products of bacteria breeding. Animals that have a crowded mouth, or a malocclusion will be more prone to gum and periodontal disease.

The chewing action serves to help naturally keep teeth clean. Chewing stimulates saliva production and the enzymes in the saliva help to break down plaque. This is why, for some animals, chewing raw meaty bones, dental bones and other rubbery chews can help to clean teeth.

If your dog is not a chewer, or is prone to chipping his teeth on bones, you may need to consider brushing the teeth with a soft child's tooth brush and some doggy toothpaste. Here is a list of handy tips to make the tooth brushing experience easier:

- *Use a soft child's toothbrush.* Forget the plastic things you slip over your finger. They don't do much as far as I have ever been able to tell, and I've been accidentally bitten several times while trying to use them!
- *Never use human tooth paste.* It is too high in fluoride and also has foaming agents in it. As dogs are not trained to 'spit' the paste out, they can swallow a dangerous amount of the soap, ending up with a tummy ache! Mint isn't the dog's ideal choice for flavour either—specially formulated dog pastes come in a variety of canine cuisine flavours—malt, chicken, biscuit, beef and cheese or prawn to name a few.
- *Start as young as you can.* First just get your dog used to you touching its mouth. Open its mouth, rub the lips and reward it for being calm. Next, use a wash cloth to wipe the mouth and teeth. You can apply something they like the taste of, such as vegemite, to make the experience more pleasant. Always reward good behaviour with a nice pat and a treat.
- *When your dog is relaxed about having its mouth examined, you can introduce the toothbrush.* The outside of the teeth, and the back teeth are the most important areas to concentrate on in most

dogs. Spend about two minutes brushing around the whole mouth, then give a reward.

For this process to work, you need to brush the teeth at least every other day.

Clipping nails

Out of all the procedures we perform routinely in a vet surgery, one of the most stressful, especially for big dogs, is nail clipping. This is the typical procedure where 'Buster' is a placid darling in the waiting room, only to turn into a rabid, biting and lunging monster at the site of a pair of nail clippers. I'll never forget the day I took the most teddy bear-like German Shepherd into the consulting room for a simple check and vaccination. 'Mr Robinson' as he was affectionately called, was putty in my hands. The liver treats went down very well, and Mr's owner and I were mutually gushing with praise at how beautiful the shepherd was as a pet. Then she politely requested I give him a minor pedicure on departure. No problem, of course.

About 10 minutes later, we emerged from the consulting room, the two of us exhausted and red faced. Mr Robinson was beside himself and the waiting room agog as I darted past into the safety of the hospital, with a giant rip down the front of my shirt—the poor dog had almost ripped the shirt clean off me in terror.

The only way to make this procedure easier on you and your pet is to start clipping nails from an early age, and do it regularly. This has many benefits. For one, it takes the stress away from the dog and owner. Secondly, it is several hundred dollars cheaper than having to book a general anaesthetic to trim down the talons.

To do a decent job of clipping toenails, you need a second person there to help restrain the dog. Have them hold the dog's head and reassure the dog while you get hold of the foot. Rest the foot on the palm of your hand and hold the toenail between your thumb and first finger. Using the clippers, clip just below the part where the hook starts. If the nail is unpigmented, you will be able to see a reddish blood vessel. Go below this.

For black nails, you just have to cut below where the hook starts and you should miss this vessel (also known as the quik). You should aim to cut straight upwards, at a 90-degree angle to the nail. This will enable you to get the nail as short as possible and minimize the risk of causing any bleeding.

If the nail does bleed…don't panic. *While a little blood goes a long way and can look frightening, no dog has ever died as a result of a bleeding toenail.* Apply some pressure, or , if you have a cake of soap handy, push the nail into this to plug the vessel. If the blood doesn't stop after five minutes, you may need to see the vet who will apply some potassium permanganate crystals, or use a cautery device to cauterize the nail bed.

Growth diets

The subject of nutrition is a very controversial one. Some people feel very strongly that dogs should be fed only a BARF diet (bones and raw food) while others are adamant that commercially prepared dry foods are the answer. The mere mention of what to feed your dog in front of some of these passionate lobbyists invokes high emotions and heated discussion.

The pet food industry is a multi-billion dollar business. Pet foods now come in all shapes and sizes. You can buy dog foods for large, small, medium breeds, for dogs in the growth phase, food for glossy coats, food specifically targeting teeth, skin, weight and even brain function and you can even buy breed specific diets for breeds such as poodles, German Shepherds and Labradors.

I have to admit, I'm a bit of a fence sitter on this subject. I certainly feel that a natural, balanced diet is excellent, and bones are good for animals which tolerate them. But as a pet owner with a busy life, like many others, I appreciate the convenience of high-quality dry food.

The human members of my family eat healthy, fresh food most days, but we still buy prepared things when we run out of time to cook. My message is, simply, feed the best you can afford and what fits into the time you have.

- Most puppies are weaned onto a varied diet or a single complete food by the time they are six to eight weeks of age.
- Contrary to popular belief, milk is not an essential diet of weaned puppies. After weaning, their ability to digest lactose becomes progressively less efficient and feeding large quantities of milk can cause diarrhoea. You can still feed it if the puppy tolerates it, in small amounts.
- Puppies should have their food allowance divided into four small meals a day until they are about 10 weeks of age, then three meals a day until they have reached approximately 50 per cent of their expected adult body weight. This is usually five to six months of age, and at this time, they can be fed twice daily.
- In general, most breeds of dog will have reached half their adult body weight by five to six months of age. Larger breeds take longer to mature than small breeds. Small and toy breeds may reach their full adult weight by the time they are six to nine months old. In contrast the large breeds such as the Labrador Retriever and newfoundland reach their adult weight at around 16 months and two years, respectively.
- Don't feed your growing dog ad libitum. If you do this, they tend to overeat, and end up obese or with skeletal and growth abnormalities. As a feeding guide, giving about 85 per cent or ad lib amounts has been shown to result in optimum growth and body composition in dogs.

Can dogs be vegetarians?

Dogs are a member of the order carnivora, but as far as nutrition goes it would be more accurate to describe them as omnivores. Although they do tend to prefer meat, dogs can actually survive happily on a vegetarian diet. If you want to consider this action, you must have veterinary supervision.

A word about supplementation

If you are feeding your puppy a balanced diet that is formulated for growth, you will not need to give any form of supplementation. Over supplementation of any nutrients can cause serious dietary imbalances and nutritional diseases.

If you give too many of the fat soluble vitamins A and D, this can result in skeletal abnormalities—care needs to be taken when giving any supplements such as cod liver oil, which is a rich source of both these vitamins. This is even true of large breeds, since their increased needs are met by their increased food intake.

How to read a pet food label

From what I see in practice, most pet owners still just blindly buy whatever stands out most on the labelling and maybe what is cheapest. Some are happiest to take their vet's recommendation and a few are concerned and confused, wanting to understand more about the contents of the food they buy. The latter group is growing, as we become more interested in what is in our own food, people are also on the look out for harmful additives and preservatives in their pet's tucker box. This is a good thing. The better the quality food you feed your pet, the longer your pet will live and the fewer visits you are likely to have to your vet.

There has been a lot of publicity in the past few years about harmful additives to pet foods. Last year there was a major recall of dog food in the United States due to a premium pet food containing contaminated wheat gluten which is used as a protein source or filler in some foods. The contaminant was identified as melamine, a chemical used in plastics manufacture and fertilizer. This lead to a lot of panic and unnecessary knee jerk reaction here, but it has served the purpose of forcing us to take notice of what's in our pet's food.

Here's a list of common terms on the label of pets foods:

Chicken, beef or fish: clean flesh from these animals.

Meat by-products: this can be blood, bone and organs such as liver, spleen, lungs brain, stomach oesophagus and other organs.

Poultry by-products: Can be undeveloped eggs, feet and necks, but not feathers

Meat or poultry by-product meal: blood, bone, and organs that are rendered dried and ground up. This can also include tissues from animals that have died outside the slaughter house.

Steamed bone meal: bones separated through cooking and ground up. It provides minerals mainly calcium and phosphorus.

Taurine: an amino acid needed by cats.

Grains: whole grains such as wheat and corn, or ground up products, which are what is left after cereals and flour is processed.

Vegetables: dried yams, beet pulp and carrots.

Additives: vitamins, minerals, flavourings and preservatives.

When you read the information panel on a label, the ingredients will be listed by weight, in descending order. This might sound simple, but it can be tricky. Firstly, if crude protein is on the list, this refers to the total protein content, and not just that which the animals can digest! You can gain a bit of good information from the list though. Animal protein based foods will be more palatable than plant protein (grain) based ones. Also, if water, grains, or meals are on the top of the ingredients list—beware, it means there's not much goodness in the food to speak of.

On the labels of cheaper dog foods, you will see things like 'animal fats'. This is low quality mix of any fats that are usually rendered at high heat—it can even include road kill or diseased animals.

Before you go running off to prepare Fido home cooked meals—that's not so easy either. If you want to do this, you need guidance from your vet or a pet nutritionist or someone very experienced. It is not as easy as you might think to balance a dog's diet.

The best advice I can offer is read labels, feed as fresh as possible, go local, avoid foods where sugar, salt, water, grains are the main ingredients and avoid foods that have a lot of preservatives in them.

Pet food label rules

In order to have some truth in labelling, the following descriptions are the general rules of the pet food industry associations.

The 95 per cent rule: if the product says 'Salmon Cat Food' or 'Beef Dog Food,' 95 per cent of the product must be the named ingredients. A product with a combination label, such as 'Beef and Liver for Dogs,' must contain 95 per cent beef and liver, and there must be more beef than liver, since beef is named first.

The 25 per cent or 'dinner' rule: ingredients named on the label must comprise at least 25 per cent of the product but less than 95 per cent, when there is a qualifying 'descriptor' term like 'dinner,' 'entree,' 'formula,' 'platter,' 'nuggets,' etc. In 'Beef Dinner for Dogs,' beef may or may not be the primary ingredient. If two ingredients are named ('Beef and Turkey Dinner for Dogs'), the two ingredients must total 25 per cent, there must be more of the first ingredient (beef) than the second (turkey), and there must be at least 3 per cent of the lesser ingredient.

The 3 per cent or 'with' rule: a product may be labelled 'Cat Food with Salmon' if it contains at least 3 per cent of the named ingredient.

The 'flavour' rule: s food may be labelled 'Turkey Flavour Cat Food' even if the food does not contain such ingredients, as long as there is a 'sufficiently detectable' amount of flavour. This may be derived from meals, by-products, or 'digests' of various parts from the animal species indicated on the label.

Fussy eaters

We humans are obsessed with food. We spend hours making it look pretty and taste great and we're very stuck on the subject of variety. That's all well and good (and I'm no less obsessed than the next person), except when we try to impose this attitude on our pets. There are some pet owners who are convinced their dog or cat needs to have a different meal every day. I had a client recently who just couldn't understand why her pet had diarrhoea all the time. On questioning, I discovered her pampered pooch was chomping through turkey, grated carrot, lettuce, cream cheese and peas on Monday, fish, prawns, chocolate milk, and vegetable medley on Tuesday, chilli con carne (!) on Wednesday, and the list goes on!! Let me tell you, *dogs are not little people. They don't need variety and nor do they necessarily like it*. In the wild, a dog might catch prey once a week. They eat the entire beast, gastrointestinal contents and all, and week after week it's usually the same thing.

Interestingly, wild dogs rarely have dental disease, are not prone to obesity, and are not fussy eaters!

If you have a fussy eater, a gradual approach, using a lot of will power usually works best. Decide on the type of diet you want your pet to eat and mix it well into the current food. Over a week, you can increase the amount until you are feeding 100 per cent of the chosen food.

Don't feed table scraps and don't panic if your pet is leaving the food. It is extremely rare for a dog to starve to death in the battle for who controls the pantry.

Many people have a problem with dogs begging at the dinner table. The answer to this is a mixture of good obedience training and common sense. If no one feeds the dog at the table, it is less likely to persist. Teach the dog that it must sit and stay out of reach while the family is eating.

A dog or cat should always be fed after the rest of the family has eaten, and preferably right away from the human eating area.

Obesity

Recent RSPCA data reveals that over 40 per cent of Aussie pooches are significantly overweight.

The best time to address weight in pets is when they are young. If you don't start bad habits in the first place, then they can't continue.

Those extra pounds could be seriously affecting your pet's health and happiness. Obesity in pets predisposes them to diabetes, heart disease, respiratory illness, cancer, arthritis and ruptured ligaments, heat and exercise intolerance and increased anaesthetic and surgery risks.

The best way to figure out if your pet is overweight is to do a body condition score. Ideally, the ribs should be easily felt, with a slight fat cover, there should be a well-defined waist and the tummy should tuck up neatly underneath. If you dog or cat scores a four or five, then it's time for some serious action!

Many veterinary hospitals have slimmers programmes. The vet or nurse will weight your pet, and work out a tailor made diet and exercise program for him. As a rule, you should aim for a one per cent weight loss each week until the target weight is achieved.

To successfully help Fido shed his pounds, you're going to have to help him break a lifetime of bad food and exercise habits. Genetics plays a small role (we all know the main aim of a Labrador and Beagle is to eat as much food and get as fat as possible in the shortest time possible!), but mostly, it's simply too much food.

Feeding tips
- Stick to the recommended daily allowance of food—even weigh the food to avoid accidental overfeeding

- Don't feed table scraps or snacks
- Divide the daily allowance into several meals
- Keep the pet away from your dinner table
- Never leave food lying around
- Introduce any new dietary food slowly over a one-week period to avoid adverse reactions.

A few things that might surprise you!

- Bones are probably the most fattening thing you can feed your dog. They are highly nutritious, and loaded with calories and usually replace a full day's calorie quota. For that reason you shouldn't give them while your pet's on a diet.
- A few biscuits or a bite of toast here and there might sound perfectly harmless, but for your dog or cat, it can be a serious setback. One small plain biscuit given to a 10kg dog is equivalent to a 163cm tall human eating an entire hamburger! So you see, if you're throwing a few bikkies at Fido while you're having your cuppa, he might be getting his entire day's needs!

Human equivalent (163cm female)	Food for a dog weighing 10kg
1 small plain biscuit	1 hamburger/1 chocolate bar
1 slice of buttered toast	1 hamburger/1 chocolate bar
100g sausage	6 iced donuts
30g cheese	1½ burgers/75g chocolate.

Once you've got your pet started on a sensible eating plan, it's time to burn a few extra calories with a good, tailor made exercise programme. Make sure you get veterinary advice on this. For dogs, try regular walks, ball throwing, jogging and cycling. Try to exercise your dog with other dogs—they love the interaction. Think about joining an agility club. Swimming and hydrotherapy (yes, there is hydrotherapy available for dogs) is great for the older arthritic pets, and even games like playing hide-and-seek with toys will get him moving. There's a real plus for us in this as well. The National Heart Foundation has released statistics that state that pet owners are 5 per cent less likely to suffer heart disease and possibly depression, than the rest of the population!

Toxic foods

Many human foods can cause problems for pets. Chocolate, onions, alcohol, and foods high in fat, sugar, or salt can be very harmful. Chocolate, coffee, and tea all contain dangerous components called 'xanthines', which cause nervous system or urinary system damage and heart muscle stimulation. Problems from ingestion of chocolate range from diarrhoea to seizures and death. All chocolate, fudge and other candy should be placed out of your dog's reach. Grapes and raisins contain an unknown toxin, which can damage the kidneys.

Chicken bones, plastic food wrap, coffee grounds, meat trimmings, the string from a roast—all pose a potential hazard. Scraps from ham or other foods high in fat can cause vomiting and diarrhoea, or pancreatitis. To be safe, put food away immediately, dog-proof your garbage, and do not feed table scraps to your dog. Uncooked meat, fish, and poultry can contain disease-causing bacteria, such as E. coli, and parasites, such as toxoplasmosis.

Uncooked foods should not be given to your dog. For your own health, as well as your pet's, wash utensils that have been in contact with raw meat, and cook meat thoroughly.

Holidays and pets

A few years ago my husband and I took Minou, along with our children to a pet friendly resort. The trip was a resounding success. Siôn and I enjoyed all the comfort of a farm stay retreat, including great food, horse riding, bushwalks and I indulged in the spa treatment with a massage and manicure. Minou was likewise in heaven—she saw horses for the first time, inspected geese and romped endlessly in the paddocks and around the dams. While she wasn't allowed to sleep inside, her accommodation on the verandah was certainly as least as good as she gets at home.

For anyone who wants to take their pet on holidays with them, I can thoroughly recommend it. There are now many places around the world that take pets, from caravan parks and camping zones, right through to five star hotels in the major cities.

Tips for taking your pet on holidays

- Find out about the local area—what diseases are prevalent there (heartworm paralysis ticks, fleas, etc). Contact your vet to find out if your pet should have any treatments before you go, or whether or take any preventative medications. Some people like to have a history to take with them.
- Get the details of the local vet at your destination.
- Contact the destination before you depart to see whether there are any special conditions you need to adhere to, such as bedding, number of or type of animals, food and water arrangements, etc.
- Make sure your pet has a collar on with an identification tag. It is a good idea to have a second tag made up, with your mobile number and the address and phone number of the place you are staying.
- Animals can easily become stressed in a new environment and this can affect their behaviour, digestive patterns and thus affect you and your pet's enjoyment of the holiday. Even little things like

a familiar blanket, toy or bed can help ease the animal into the new surroundings. You should consider visiting the vet before taking your pet on holiday. The vet can do a check-up of the animal's health, recommend any vaccinations required for the area you are visiting and provide you with a printout of your pet's medical history in case of an emergency.

- Respect the rules of your travelling destination, especially regarding your pet. It is a privilege to take your furry companion on holiday with you and the better behaved the pet, the more likely accommodation venues across the country will open their doors to animals.

If you are not planning on taking your pet on vacation with you, you will need to make arrangements for the care of your pet while you are away. There are a few different options here, including boarding kennels, house sitters and people who will take your dog into their own home.

Boarding options

Vet clinics

Some vet hospitals and clinics will board dogs and cats. If you have an elderly dog, or a sick dog, this can be the ideal situation as a vet will always be on hand to conduct a clinical examination if needs be.

Check on how much attention and exercise the dog will get and ask to see the boarding facilities.

Dog sitters

These people will either stay in your house while you are away, or call in frequently to ensure your pet is okay. Having a pet sitter stay over has many benefits, including greater security from burglars and giving the pet company for more hours of the day, keeping him more settled, as well as someone to collect the mail, put the rubbish out and the little day-to-day things.

Before you enter into an agreement with a pet sitter, you need to make sure they are both trustworthy and 'on the same page' as you in terms of expectations. Here is a list of things to take note of and some possible questions to ask:

- How does the person relate to pets?
- If the person cannot stay at the house, how often will they be able to call around (three times a day is recommended, depending on the health of your pet)?
- Will they be prepared to do other things such as collect mail and the newspaper?
- How much will they charge?
- Do they know how to give medications and will they be prepared to do this?
- Can they restrain the pet and are they able to take it for walks and groom it if necessary?
- How much experience do they have? Can they provide references?
- Are they familiar with the local vet?
- Are they dog savvy? For example, what would they do if the dog had diarrhoea for a few days in a row, or was vomiting, or listless?

If you are using a house sitter, make sure you go through your expectations thoroughly; these include the house and garden as well as the dog. Let the sitter know vets details and contact your vet to make an arrangement for treatment of your pet in your absence.

Boarding at someone else's house

Some people will take a few pets into their own home to look after them. There are several companies that manage these services. This can be very successful, particularly as many of these people are at home all day, and most will allow your pet to have its own belongings with it and to live as it does at home (eg, indoors or outdoors or both). If several dogs are boarding together, the boarding host will probably also screen the dogs to make sure they all get along.

You will have the opportunity to visit the home your pet is going to, and you should ask the same questions as for the boarding kennel.

Boarding kennels

This is the most popular and possibly the most owner-friendly alternative. Boarding kennels take on many animals and they are generally housed in some type of kennel arrangement. Kennels can differ hugely in the type of accommodation and facilities they offer and different kennels will appeal to different owners and animals. Some kennels offer basic undercover shelters for pets at night, and have the pets running free in a fenced paddock during the day. Other facilities have a kennel attached to a small dog run, which might be shared between two dogs. Some kennels are 100 per cent indoors unless you pay extra to have the dog taken outdoors for exercise. Other boarding situations are quite luxurious, with dogs staying in mini 'houses' complete with beds and televisions and a CCTV facility where you can watch them over the internet.

Make sure you research your choices thoroughly. Have an inspection of the kennel. I would not board my dog at any kennel I had not seen.

Here are some questions to ask boarding kennels:

- What are the sizes of the kennels or runs? Do they have solid partitions between them? Are there both indoor and outdoor facilities?
- How frequently, where, and for how long are the dogs walked?
- Are the kennels, runs, and exercise areas clean and free from excrement? Does the kennel or exercise area smell?
- How often are the kennels, dishes cleaned, and with what? How are the kennels cleaned between boarders?
- Which vaccinations are required, and which are recommended?

Are vaccinations that you administered acceptable or do they need to be given by a veterinarian?

- Will they bathe your dog if he becomes soiled with urine or excrement?
- What is the regular feeding schedule, and can it be adapted if your dog has special needs? Can you bring the dog's regular food?
- Who actually works with the animals?
- What are their admit and pick up hours? What if your return is delayed?
- Is there a veterinarian or emergency clinic nearby? Can you use your own veterinarian?
- Is there a time you can call to check on how your dog is doing?
- What are their security provisions? Do the kennels and cages have good latches? Are the fences to the outdoor runs at least six feet high?
- Is the facility accredited by a boarding kennel association? These members must abide by a strict code of ethics which demonstrates their professionalism and high standards.

As with finding other providers, ask your vet, family, and friends for their recommendations when choosing a boarding facility. Regardless of the boarding facility/sitter you decide on, make reservations far in advance, if possible. Many facilities are fully booked four to six months in advance for times such as Christmas or Easter.

6

BREED PROFILES

Afghan Hound

Afghans are huge, elegant, strong and dignified dogs. They were originally bred as a hunting dog. This breed need a good deal of exercise each day, and are happier kept in a large yard or acreage. Afghan hounds have a long silky coat that requires daily grooming for maintenance.

This breed can be quite aloof, especially with strangers. They are also an independent character, making them a challenge to train. A great pet for those who are prepared to put the work in.

Height 60–74cm (24–29in) **Weight** 23–30kg (50–66lb)
Exercise **** **Grooming** ***

Airedale terrier

The Airedale terrier is the largest of the terrier breed and also one of the most versatile. These dogs have been used as hunters, retrievers, pit fighters herders, police dogs, guide dogs and even messengers and sentry during the first world war.

Airedale terriers are loyal companions, patient with children and easy to train. They are best kept as only dogs, or with another dog of the opposite sex to prevent fighting.

This is an energetic breed that need plenty of exercise and their coat required regular clipping.

Height 56–61cm (22–24in) **Weight** 20–26kg (44–57lb)
Exercise **** **Grooming** ***

Akita Inu

The Akita is an imposing looking dog, with a massive chest and thick coarse coat, as well as a powerful head, which gives it the look of a bear. This is the national dog of Japan.

The Akita is a fearless, dignified and somewhat aloof animal that makes an excellent, no nonsense guard dog, but needs to be supervised around children and visitors, and are often aggressive towards other dogs.

Not a pet for everyone, this breed need good obedience training and early socialisation if they are going to have a reliable temperament.

Height 61–71cm (24–28in)   **Weight** 40–48kg (88–105lb)
Exercise ****   **Grooming** **

Alaskan Malamute

Malamutes were bred by the inuit Indians of Alaska to pull sleds carrying heavy loads across long distances in a harsh climate. The Malamute is a large powerful dog with a luxurious, thick coat and beautiful markings. These dogs have a naturally curious, playful temperament. They crave exercise and if they don't get it, they can be destructive and end up being labelled 'crazy'.

These dogs tend to be too social and friendly to be guard dogs. They are a wonderful, gentle family pet although obedience training can be challenging. Lack of confident, firm human domination can ruin an otherwise wonderful Malamute making it domineering over humans and unmanageably aggressive toward other dogs.

Height 58–63cm (23–25in)   **Weight** 34–40kg (75–88kg)
Exercise ****   **Grooming** ***

Australian Cattle dog

The Australian Cattle dog was 'made in Australia', bred by Australian stockmen who knew what they wanted in a cattle dog and set about producing it.Even as pets, these dogs retain their protective nature and herding instincts. They are excellent watch dogs but do need supervision around children.

Cattle dogs are an extremely active breed and need regular, vigorous exercise and obedience training as well as socialisation with both humans and other canines. If cattle dogs do not receive sufficient mental and physical stimulation, they can become bored, destructive and domineering. Suitable for active people.

Height 38–51cm (15–20in)	**Weight** 23–27kg (51–60lb)
Exercise ****	**Grooming** *

The Australian Kelpie

The Australian Kelpie has a natural instinct and aptitude for the working of sheep, both in open country or in yards, and is renowned for the way in which he runs over the sheep's backs.

A tough, independent, highly intelligent dog with extreme loyalty and utmost devotion to duty, the Australian Kelpie has a tractable disposition. Obedient and super alert, he is eager to please and makes a devoted companion, however his inexhaustible energy makes him unsuitable for suburban living.

Kelpies must be well exercised or they can become frustrated and destructive. This breed idolizes their owner, are highly motivated to play and are always ready for a game. Their high activity levels can make them hard to control and they should be supervised around young children.

Height 43–51cm (17–20in)	**Weight** 16–20kg (35–44lb)
Exercise ****	**Grooming** *

Australian Silky Terrier

The Australian Silky Terrier, or 'Sydney Silky' as he is often known, was bred here in Australia as a cross between the Aussie terrier and the Yorkie. Early Sydneysiders needed a dog which was small enough to live in a small home, but an excellent hunter of vermin. Silkies look glamorous and delicate with their silky coat and fine build but they are actually a true terrier with plenty of spunk and 'get up and go'.

They make excellent watch dogs and love children.

Height up to 23cm (9in)   **Weight** 3.5–4.5kg (7.5–10lb)
Exercise **   **Grooming** **

Australian Terrier

This proud, Aussie breed was developed as the result of crossing various British Terriers that were brought to Australia by the first settlers. The Australian Terrier is a true blue Australian all-rounder, as he's used for a variety of work including killing rats and snakes, tending sheep, and guarding farms and mines.

While Australian Terriers started out as a working dog, their affectionate personality has resulted in a very popular companion dog.

Australian Terriers are renowned for their intelligence, loyalty and their reliable temperament. They make excellent guard dogs and are happy to live indoors or out. A spunky, endearing companion.

Height up to 25cm (10in)   **Weight** approx. 6.5kg (14.5lb)
Exercise **   **Grooming** *

Basenji

These elegant dogs have their origins in the African Congo and were introduced to Europe in 1870. The Basenji is renowned for the fact that they do not bark. They still make plenty of noise though, with a variety of sounds in their repertoire, including chortles, yodels and growls.

The Basenji is a happy, sensitive dog. They love people but are not necessarily openly affectionate. They are a highly inquisitive and curious breed which is entertaining but can make them difficult to train.

They are fastidiously clean, and groom themselves with their tongue, like a cat.

Height 40–43cm (15.5–17in)	**Weight** 9.5–11kg (21–24lb)
Exercise ***	**Grooming** *

Basset Hound

Basset Hounds are extremely affectionate and gentle dogs. They are tolerant and gentle, and great with children.

These dogs are popular pets, partly because of their appealing looks and perfect medium size, but also due to their perennially sunny disposition and lazy nature at home.

Bassets are actually natural athletes, endowed with exceptional physical strength and endurance. These are the first hunting dogs. They are driven by their noses and love to be out in the field, following a scent.

Bassets need plenty of exercise, or they can become serial escape artists. Because of their stubborn streak, they can be challenging to train.

While they are a short statured dog, they are very long and large, so they should not be considered for owners who want a 'small' dog.

Height 33–38cm (13–15in)	**Weight:** 23–28kg (51–62lb)
Exercise ***	**Grooming** **

Beagle

The Beagle is a very popular dog, partly because of its good looks and perennially sunny disposition but also because of its perfect medium size and its appealing playful wit.

Beagles are lively, active dogs that can adapt to suburban backyards provided they get adequate training and exercise. They make devoted pets, and are great with both children and adults.

These dogs are a pack oriented hunting hound, and therefore prone to roaming, especially if they don't get the exercise and stimulation they require.

Height 33–41cm (13–16in)	**Weight** 12–14kg (26.5–31lb)
Exercise **	**Grooming** *

Bearded Collie

The 'Beardie' is one of Britain's oldest breeds. He was highly prized as a sheepherding dog in Scotland and also has excellent cattle-droving ability. These dogs have a luxurious long, flat coat which requires regular grooming. The coat comes in a variety of colours including slate grey, red, black and blue.

Bearded Collies are excellent family dogs. They adore romping with the kids, and will be a contented family dog as long as they get ample opportunity for exercise.

Height 51–56cm (20–22in)	**Weight** 19–25kg (42–55lb)
Exercise ****	**Grooming** ***

Bedlington Terrier

The Bedlington Terrier gets its name from the Northumberland country in England, where it was originally kept by miners and gypsies for hunting foxes, badger and other vermin.

With time, the attractive, unmistakably lamb like appearance of the Bedlington made it a popular pet of the elite.

Bedlingtons are very affectionate and unfailingly loyal to their family, but they can be jealous and are often aggressive towards other dogs. They are very responsive to training and are a good pet for most age groups. Bedlington Terriers have a non shedding coat which is thick and linty and has a tendency to twist. They do need regular grooming and clipping to keep them comfortable.

Height 41cm (16in)   **Weight** 8.2–10.4kg (18–23lb)
Exercise **   **Grooming** ****

Belgian Shepherd Dog

Belgian Shepherds have an instinctive herding ability, as they were originally bred in Europe for use as a herding dog. They are an intelligent breed, being attentive to their owners and easy to train. Their highly trainable nature saw them used during World War 1 as trained messengers. Today they are used for police work throughout Europe. The breed now has four distinctive types which are named according to the district they originated: The Groenendael, Tervueren, Malinois, and Laekenois. These types vary in coat colour and length.

Belgian Shepherds excel at obedience work and make a loyal family companion but their naturally protective instincts mean they need to be socialized at an early age and always supervised around visiting adult and children.

Height 58–62cm (23–24.5in)   **Weight** 30–36kg (66–79lb)
Exercise **   **Grooming** **

Bernese Mountain Dog

These dogs are strikingly attractive for their large size and beautiful coat colour and markings. They were originally brought to Switzerland by the invading Romans over 2000 years ago, and by the early 1900s, were almost extinct. A fanciers club started a breed rehabilitation program and the Bernese, originally used as a drover's dog and a watch, is now a popular house pet and companion in Switzerland and around the world.

Bernese have a medium length, silky coat which requires a moderate amount of grooming. They are extremely friendly, self confident and fearless but not aggressive. In order to make good pets, they need plenty of attention and involvement from the family.

Height 58–70cm (23–27.5in)	**Weight** 34–49 kg (75–108lb)
Exercise **	**Grooming** **

Bichon Frise

Descendants of the Bichon Frise were brought to Europe from the Canary Islands in the early fourteenth century. Bichons were originally an item or barter, but then became a favourite pet of the European aristocracy.

Bichons have had centuries of dependence on humans (*bichon* is French for *lap dog*) and as a result, they have a strong sense of belonging in a family. They are remarkably affectionate, intelligent, easy to train, confident and optimistic.

They have a fluffy, white non shedding coat that does require regular brushing and grooming.

Height less than 30cm (12in)	**Weight**: 5kg (11lb)
Exercise *	**Grooming** ***

Bloodhound

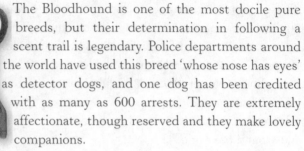

The Bloodhound is one of the most docile pure breeds, but their determination in following a scent trail is legendary. Police departments around the world have used this breed 'whose nose has eyes' as detector dogs, and one dog has been credited with as many as 600 arrests. They are extremely affectionate, though reserved and they make lovely companions.

Bloodhounds must have regular, daily exercise or else they will become bored. They are an intelligent breed and they do learn quickly, but can be obstinate in formal training. Anyone considering a Bloodhound will need to keep in mind their huge size, food requirements and short average lifespan.

Height 58–69cm (23–27in)	**Weight** 36–50kg (66–110lb)
Exercise ****	**Grooming** **

Border Collie

The Border Collie was very much developed in Australia, but they derive their name from the border between Scotland and England where they originated. Border Collies are one of the world's best sheep dogs, able to run more than 80km a day and do the work of several men. They are also highly intelligent, brilliant performers in the obedience ring and loyal, devoted companions to their master.

Border Collies have high energy requirements and unless they have extensive daily exercise, with activities such as ball chasing, they can become noisy and destructive.Because of their strong herding instinct, they must be supervised around children.

Height 46–53cm (18–21in)	**Weight** approx 23kg (51lb)
Exercise ****	**Grooming** **

Border Terrier

Border terriers were originally bred to hunt and kill the foxes that were ravaging sheep flocks in the Cheviot Hills region of Great Britain.

Borders are a strong, active, tireless breed, alert and very agile. These dogs have a wiry, resistant top coat with a short dense undercoat. Colours include tan, grizzle, red, blue or wheaten.

Border terriers are good natures, affectionate dogs that make excellent pets. They are easily trained.

Height 32.5–37.5cm (13–15in)   **Weight** 5–7kg (11–15.5lb)
Exercise **   **Grooming**. **

Borzoi

The Borzoi was originally bred by the Russian aristocracy for the sole purpose of wolf hunting. They are an agile, swift and courageous dog, but also tall, slender and haughty looking, making them one of the most noble, elegant breeds.

Borzois need a lot of exercise to keep them fit, and while they are affectionate with their owner, they are aloof and distrustful of strangers. They can be a challenging breed to obedience train, but they are quiet, gentle dogs who love to live as part of the family. They need to be supervised around young children and smaller pets.

Height 68cm–74cm (27–29in)   **Weight** 33kg (73lb)
Exercise: ****   **Grooming:** **

Boston Terrier

The Boston Terrier was originally developed as a cross between the British Bulldog and white English Terrier, as a fighting dog in Boston.

This breed is now a gentle, peaceful dog. They are good with children and are bright, alert, obedient and easy to care for. Bostons can be strong willed and determined, so obedience training takes patience.

They make excellent watch dogs, but are too small to be effective guard dogs.

Height not specified	**Weight**: 6.8–11.4kg (15–25lb)
Exercise **	**Grooming** *

Bouvier Des Flandres

The Bouvier Des Flanders is a powerful, large dog with a rugged appearance that was originally bred as a cattle dog in the northern hills of France. This breed is a highly prized police dog and defence dog is Europe and has also been used as a tracking dog, and guide dog for the blind.

Bouviers are intelligent, energetic and audacious. They thrive on a active lifestyle and need plenty of exercise to keep them happy.

The Bouviers Des Flanders makes an excellent watch dog and guard dogs, because although they are exceptionally loving and docile with their owners, they are distinctly suspicious of strangers.

Height 59–68cm (23–26.5in)	**Weight** 27–40kg (59–88lb)
Exercise ****	**Grooming** **

Boxer

Surprisingly, the Boxer was virtually unheard of outside Germany until the 1940s. At the end of the World War II, American and British soldiers took these dogs home with them, and they became immediately popular.

The Boxer is the clown of the guard dogs. He takes his guarding job very seriously, but is always ready to play—even in old age. These dogs are happy and affectionate by nature, but they can also be stubborn and need a no nonsense, gentle training routine to keep them in check.

Boxers are clean quiet, excellent family dogs that usually love children and adults alike. They have boundless energy and need plenty of exercise, without which they can become boisterous and unruly.

Height 53–61cm (21–24in) **Weight** 25–32kg (55–70lb)
Exercise **** **Grooming** *

Briard

The Briard was originally a superior French sheep dog and guard dog. It became the official dog of the French army during World War I, where many died carrying supplies to the front line, or working as sentrys.

The Briard has a distinctive teddy bear like appearance with a coarse, rough coat, distinctive beard and moustache and dark eyes hidden by tufts of hair. His coat needs regular grooming, is medium length and wavy.

Briards are a good natured, fun loving dog. They are boisterous and outgoing and require consistent careful training from a young age if they are to be a well controlled pet. Great with kids and adults alike.

Height 56–68cm (22–27) **Weight** 34–41kg (75–90lb)
Exercise *** **Grooming** ***

British Bulldog

With its imposing build, muscular shoulders, enormous head and chest and tremendous weight for its height, many consider the British Bulldog to be the most distinguished of all canines. The British have chosen the Bulldog to symbolize the qualities Britons display in their finest moments—courage, tenacity and equanimity.

Originally, these dogs were set against bulls in the once popular sport of 'bull baiting'. Today they are an excellent children's companion and household pet.

They are loyal and dependable but have an obstinate streak that needs careful training to achieve a well mannered dog.

Height 41cm (16in)	**Weight** 22.7–25kg (50–55lb)
Exercise *	**Grooming** *

Bull Terrier

The Bull Terrier was once known as the gladiator of the canine world, bred for its prowess in the dog fight pits. These days, however, he is regarded as a true gentleman, being the kindest of dogs towards people, displaying a soft benevolent attitude and thriving on human affection.

This breed is still inherently aggressive towards other dogs, and best as an only dog in the household.

Bull Terriers are an extremely strong, tenacious breed that need a good deal of exercise. They can be very stubborn so need firm obedience training.

Height 43–53cm (17–21lb)	**Weight** 20–30kg (44–66lb)
Exercise ***	**Grooming** *

Bullmastiff

The Bullmastiff is the result of a cross between the British Bulldog and the Mastiff. They were originally bred to catch and pin down poachers in England.

This is an independent, imposing-looking breed, which needs good obedience training. Bullmastiffs, despite their size, can be gentle, clownish pets that adore the company of children. Training is a must for this breed.

Height 61–73cm (24–29in)	**Weight** 45–60kg (99–132lb)
Exercise **	**Grooming** *

Cairn Terrier

The Cairn Terrier is the smallest of the British working terriers. Cairn Terriers were originally bred to be used by the Lairds and Croftans for hunting and killing vermin, such as foxes, otters and badgers.

Cairns make a fabulous mini watch dog. They are a tough, hardy and active little animal, known for their fearlessness and independence

Cairn are easy to groom and happy with a daily run and lots of family time.

Height 28–31cm (11–12in)	**Weight** 6–7.5kg (13–16.5lb)
Exercise **	**Grooming** **

Cavalier King Charles Spaniel

King Charles 11 is the namesake of this breed. He is believed to have surrounded himself with these dogs, preferring their company to that of his courtiers.

Cavaliers are the largest of the toy dog breeds. They are lively and quite robust, being happy in children's games and loving a romp in the park.

These dogs have been domesticated for centuries, and as a result, adapt naturally to living inside. They are affectionate, gentle, friendly and have a great love for people. An ideal family pet.

Height 36cm (14in)	**Weight** 5.4–8kg (12–17.5lb)
Exercise ***	**Grooming** *

Chihuahua

The Chihuahua comes in a long coat variety, and a smooth (short) coat. This is the world's smallest dog, thought to have originated during the Aztec times and found their way to Mexico during the Spanish conquest. They were officially discovered in Mexico in the late nineteenth century.

Chihuahuas are fiercely alert and hyper-protective. They make good watch dogs. They love adults but can be a little intimidated by young children and rough games.

Ideal size less than 2.7kg (6lb)	
Exercise *	**Grooming** *

Chow Chow

The Chow is a very ancient breed with a rather depressing history. They were initially bred as the 'Cantonese butcher's dog', their tasty meat considered a delicacy. When the British discovered them, they displayed them in zoos.

The Chow Chows is lion like to look at. They are a very large build, and have a thick, two-ply golden coat, with a big ruff around their neck.

Chows are strong willed with a stubborn streak. They do not make friends quickly, but once you win them over, they'll love you for life. These dogs can be stubborn and obstinate, and need good obedience training. They tend not to like children, and are often a 'one person' dog.

Height 46–56cm (18–22in)	**Weight:** 25–40kg (55–88lb)
Exercise *	**Grooming** **

Clumber Spaniel

The Clumber Spaniel gets its name from Clumber Park, the name of the Duke of Newcastle's estate. He apparently bred spaniels that were given to him by the French aristocrats. This breed was a popular gun dog in the eighteenth century.

Clumber Spaniels have characteristic lemon markings on a pristine white, dense coat.

The Clumber Spaniel has a gentle, calm and playful nature and makes a lovely family pet.

Height: 45–50cm (17.5–19.5in)	**Weight** 29.5–36kg (65–79.5lb)
Exercise *	**Grooming** *

Cocker Spaniel

Cocker Spaniels were originally used to flush out woodcock from the thick hedgerows, and, as good swimmers, to retrieve the game from marshlands. Cocker Spaniels are the smallest member of the gun dog family, but are more well known now as a popular family pet.

This breed is friendly, sensitive, highly intelligent and eager to please. They adore children and love to be included as part of the family.

Cockers need to be kept fit with plenty of exercise. Their silky coat needs regular grooming.

Height 38–41cm (15–16in)	**Weight** 12.75–14.5kg (28–32lb)
Exercise ***	**Grooming** **

American Cocker Spaniel

The American and English Cocker Spaniel started out as the same breed, but became so diversified after World War II that they were declared a separate entity from one another.

Like the English Cocker, these dogs are real athletes that need regular exercise. They are noted for their love and faithfulness to their master and family.

American Cockers need plenty of exercise and mental stimulation. They differ from the English Cocker mainly in build and looks. These dogs make an ideal family pet.

Height 35.5–38cm (14–15in)	**Weight** 12kg (26.5lb)
Exercise ***	**Grooming** ***

Collie

Rough Collies were, for centuries, known only in the Scottish Lowlands, where they guarded over large flocks of sheep. In 1860, Queen Victoria fell in love with the breed while taking a holiday in Scotland, and brought several Collies back to Windsor castle with her.

Collies are a highly strung, anxious breed. They are eager to please, nervous of strangers and very affectionate with children. These dogs are very easy to train and make excellent police dogs and guide dogs as well as family pets.

They shed often and their coat matts easily, so they will need regular brushing.

Height 55–66cm (21.5–26in)	**Weight** 18–29.5kg (40–65lb)
Exercise ***	**Grooming** ***

Smooth Collie

The Smooth Collie is identical to the Rough Collie except for its short, dense coat. This breed were use primarily as a drover's dog for guiding sheep and cattle to market and as such, didn't need the profuse coat of the Rough, that stood over flocks at pasture.

Like all working dogs, the Smooth Collie needs plenty of exercise and is very responsive to training.

Height 55–66cm (21.5–26in)	**Weight** 18-34kg (40–75lb)
Exercise ***	**Grooming** *

Curly Coated Retriever

The oldest of the English Retrievers, the Curly Coated Retriever was originally a gamekeeper's gun dog and guard dog. They are natural swimmers and are well renowned for swimming in cold water, at any time of the year.

This breed has a distinctive curly, waterproof coat, with a mass of dense curls extending from the back of their head to the tip of the tail. Although the Curly Coated Retriever is harder to train than the other Retriever breeds, it is a kind hearted, fun loving dog, which enjoys the company of children and loves to 'play the clown'.

Height 63.5–68.5cm (25–27in) **Weight** 36kg (79.5lb)
Exercise **   **Grooming** *

Dachshund

Dachshund is the German word for Badger dog. This breed was originally bred as a hunter and as a result, despite their small size, they display extraordinary endurance and courage.

'Daksies' are a mischievous and affectionate companion pet. They are intelligent and can be easy to   train,   as long as you keep their stubborn streak in check.

Dachshunds are prone to spine injuries because of their long, low slung bodies, and should be kept lean to minimize the risk of this. They are a great breed for a family pet, preferring gentle children.

There are six recognized breeds of dachshund, based on coat type and size: the Smooth-haired, Long-haired, Wire-haired, each in a standard or miniature size.

Standard:
Height 24cm (9.5in) **Weight** standard 9–12 kg (20–26.5lb)
Exercise *   **Grooming** *

Miniature:
Height 13–15cm (5–6in)   **Weight** miniature 4.5kg (10lb)
Exercise *   **Grooming** *

Dalmation

Everyone knows the darling Dalmatian. Its distinctive black and white spotted coat makes it the most easily recognized of all breeds.

Dalmatians were once working dogs, employed as carriage dogs to run alongside horses under the axels of carriages, protecting the occupants from being attacked by highwaymen. They actually have a broad history as a war dog and even a hunting dog!

Dalmations are strong, muscular dogs with great endurance. Their one love in life is exercise, exercise and more exercise! They are an affectionate, easily trained pet, and a sensible, dependant guard dog, but are suited best to people with a very active lifestyle.

Height 56–61cm (22–24in)   **Weight** 32kg (70.5lb)
Exercise ****   **Grooming** *

Dandie Dinmont Terrier

The Dandie Dinmont Terrier has its origins in Scotland, where it was owned by the Gypsies of the 18th century. Back then it was called the 'Pepper and Mustard' Terrier, but was renamed by Sir Walter Scott in his 1814 novel Guy Mannering.

An excellent guard dog, but also exceptionally good with children, it is very gentle and affectionate.

Height 20–28cm (7.5–11in)	**Weight** 8–11kg (17.5–24.5lb)
Exercise **	**Grooming** ***

Deerhound

The Deerhound is a huge, imposing-looking animal with very noble origins. He was once known as the royal dog of Scotland—there was, in fact, a time when the law in Scotland stated that no person below the rank of earl could keep a Deerhound.

Deerhounds were revered for their courage and tenacity as hunters of stags, but also their loyalty and faithfulness to the Highland chieftans and their kin.

Deerhounds, despite their huge size, fit comfortably into a family situation and are a special favourite with children. They need plenty of exercise.

Height 71–76cm (28–30in)	**Weight** 36.5–45.5kg (80.5–100lb)
Exercise ****	**Grooming** *

Elkhound

The Norwegian Elkhound is another hunting dog, employed to hunt for elk and alert the hunter to the elk's presence with its high pitched whimper. The elkhound was also bred as a companion to the Vikings.

The Elkhound is a lively, energetic breed, very intelligent and quick to learn. They make an ideal companion for adults and older children.

Height 49–52cm (19–20.5in)   **Weight** 20–23kg (44–51lb)
Exercise **   **Grooming** *

Doberman

The Doberman breed was developed by a German tax collector named Herr Louis Doberman. He needed a companion dog to protect him while he was doing his rounds, and because he also ran the local animal shelter, he had ample stock to breed from.

The Doberman is unparalleled as a guard dog and watch dog. He is also one of the most steadfastly devoted family companions. Because he thrives on the role of family policeman, he should be supervised around visiting children. 'Dobies' are easy to train-and this needs to start, along with socialisation, at an early age.

Height 65–69cm (25.5–27in)   **Weight** 30–33kg (66–73lb)
Exercise **   **Grooming** *

English Setter

The English Settter is a lovely breed, it was originally designed to point at game so sportsmen could line it up for their nets. These dogs are one of the most appealing breeds both in terms of temperament and appearance. They have a lovable, gentle nature and are eager to please.

Setters are happy, friendly and affectionate. They don't make good guard dogs, simply because they are likely to welcome any stranger into the house as a long lost friend!

The English Setter makes a wonderful family pet, best suited to active people or someone who lives on an acreage.

Height 61–68cm (24–27in)	**Weight** 25–38kg (55–84lb)
Exercise ****	**Grooming** *

English Springer Spaniel

The English Springer is thought to be the most robust of all the Spaniels, and also the most pleasant natured.

As a result of their legacy of their hunting, retrieving and pointing days, the Springer Spaniel is a superb all round sporting dog. It loves to run, to retrieve and to swim.

Predictably the Springer needs plenty of exercise to keep him happy. These dogs are patient and affectionate with children. They are reserved with strangers, and make very good watch dogs.

Height 48–51cm (19–20in)	**Weight** 22–25kg (48.5–55lb)
Exercise ****	**Grooming** **

Finnish Spitz

The Finnish Spitz was first used as a hunting dog in Finland and is now a common breed throughout Finland and Sweden.

This breed is lively, active and fun loving. They love people, including children, and also get along well with other pets.

They make great guard dogs and need good training.

Height 38–51cm (15-20in)	**Weight** 14–16kg (31–35lb)
Exercise ****	**Grooming** *

Flat Coated Retriever

The Flat Coated Retriever was developed in the late 18th century for retrieving game. The breed came out of crosses with sheepdogs for trainability, setters for a keen nose, spaniels for their hunting prowess and waterdogs for retrieving.

The Retriever is forever a child as they are more outgoing and fun loving than other breeds of similar size and traits, such as the Golden Retriever and the Labrador. It needs training and craves human company. Not an ideal guard dog but a wonderful companion.

Flat Coated Retrievers love to play and retrieve and adore being showered with attention.

Height 58.5–62cm (23–24.5in)	**Weight** 23–31kg (50–68.5lb)
Exercise ***	**Grooming** *

Foxhound (English)

Foxhounds were bred in England, strictly for hunting. As a result, they a pack oriented dog with incredible stamina and ability to follow a scent trail. They an eager working dog, with boundless energy and a commanding bark.

Foxhounds are a courageous, cheerful dog that enjoys the company of other dogs! Arguably not suited to city life.

Height 50–59cm (20–23.5in)   **Weight** 25–45kg (53–99lb)
Exercise ****   **Grooming** *

Fox Terrier

There are two breeds of Fox Terrier, the only difference being one has a wiry coat and the other a smooth coat.

Although originally a hunting dog, they are now bred chiefly as a companion pet. They are an adaptable pet, happy in both city and country situations. Foxys bond well with their family and make a loyal, devoted pet as well as an excellent watch dog.

Height 30–39cm (12–15in)   **Weight** 6.75–8.25kg (14.75–18lb)
Exercise **   **Grooming** *

French Bulldog

The origins of this quirky little dog is uncertain, with the French claiming is as their national breed, and the British considering them to be a descendant of the British Bulldog, which arrived in France in the 1850s. These sturdy little dogs are affectionate and courageous. They love human company and are also compatible with most other dogs. They are great with older children.

Height 28–30cm (11–12in)   **Weight** 11–13kg (60.5–85lb)
Exercise ***   **Grooming** *

German Shepherd Dog

The German Shepherd is on of the most
popular breeds of dog in the world. This dog has
contributed widely to human society as a sheep dog,
companion dog, guide dog, police dog, army dog
and guard dog.

German Shepherds are immensely versatile and can be trained in
almost any role. They make a lovely family pet when well socialized
from a young age.

Height 60–65cm (23.5–25.5in)   **Weight** 27.5–38.5kg (60.5–85lb)
Exercise ***   **Grooming** *

German Shorthaired Pointer

German Shorthaired Pointers were bred to be one of the best all-round
hunting dogs, excellent as a hunter of grouse and pheasant.

Pointers are highly intelligent and love to be obedience trained from
a young age. Because of their intelligence, if they are not trained, they
will try and dominate their masters.

Even though the Pointer has a strong personality, it is very amiable
and loves children and family. These dogs require a lot of exercise and
become unsettled and disobedient when they are not kept active.

Height 53–65cm (21–25.5in)   **Weight** 20.5–31kg (45–68lb)
Exrecise ****   **Grooming** *

Golden Retriever

Goldens are hardy, well-built dogs, originally bred to retrieve waterfowl. These dogs have a highly developed scenting ability, and are natural Retrievers, delighting in returning things to their masters.

Golden Retrievers are notably calm, gentle, loyal dogs, which make an ideal family companion. They have infinite patience with children.

Height 51–61cm (20–24in)   **Weight** 27.25–36.25kg (60–71lb)
Exercise ***   **Grooming** **

Gordon Setter

The Gordon Setter is the largest and most powerful of all the 'setters'. Gordons are heavy, strong dogs, that are not necessarily fast but have great endurance and stamina. They were popular setting dogs because they could run all day without even needing a drink.

Gordon Setters need to be exercised regularly. They make great family pets because they are gentle and affectionate. This breed is loyal to its immediate family, but reserved with strangers.

Height 58–69cm (23–27in)   **Weight** 20.5–34kg (45–75lb)
Exercise ****   **Grooming** **

Great Dane

Despite its name, the Great Dane did not have its origins in Denmark. They are thought to have been around as long as 3000 B.C. owned by the Egyptians. The modern day Dane was bred in Germany, so it is likely that the invading Romans brought the Great Dane forebearers with them to Germany in the first century.

Due to their large size, Danes are a popular guard dog. With careful training and plenty of socialisation from a young age, with both people and other dogs, Great Danes make lovely pets. They are patient with

children and affectionate with their masters.

Danes need plenty of exercise. If they are not properly socialized or trained, they can be impatient with other dogs.

Height 71–76cm (28–30in) **Weight**45.5–54.5kg (100–120lb)
Exercise *** **Grooming** *

Greyhound

The Greyhound is one of the oldest pure breeds of dog in existence. It is often depicted in Egyptian sculptures and pictures dating back at least 5000 years. This dog has always been a prized hunter, able to outpace fox and hare.

These days, Greyhounds are used mainly as sporting dogs, racing each other to catch a 'rabbit decoy'. Few people know that these dogs actually make lovely, gentle, affectionate pets that love children and get along with most other pets.

In Australia, several groups of Greyhound lovers run special adoption program where you can adopt a retired or failed greyhound.

Height 68–76cm (26.5–30in) **Weight** 27–32kg (59.5–70.5lb)
Exercise *** **Grooming** *

Griffon Bruxellois

Griffons were originally used to catch rats in stables where the hansom cabs were kept. Towards the end of the nineteenth century, these quirky looking dogs became a favourite of the royal Belgian court, and attracted British interest as well.

These dogs are inquisitive, often impertinent and always watchful. They need attentive training or they may yap or bully. They make great companion dogs. They are suitable for adults and families with older or gentle children.

Height 18–20.5cm (7–8in)   **Weight** 2.25–5.5kg (5–12lb)
Exercise *   **Grooming** *

Irish Setter

The Irish Setter is a prized pointing dog with the most spectacular and extraordinary coat colour of all breeds. The beautiful red, glossy fur and lighter coloured undercoat is judged very strictly in show rings.

These dogs are energetic and tenacious but have a tendency to be very independent and are naturally highly strung. These characteristics make them rather challenging to train.

They must get plenty of exercise to prevent them from becoming 'hyperactive' and as long as they do, they make lovely pets.

Height 64–69cm (25–27in)   **Weight** 27–32kg (59.5–70.5lb)
Exercise ****   **Grooming** *

Irish Terrier

Irish terriers are spirited daredevils of dogs. Their spritely personality along with the fiery red colour of their coat ahs earned them the nickname of 'red devil' and 'wild Irishman'.

Irish terriers are lovely, soft mouthed dogs. They make excellent guard dogs. They are not always fond of other dogs, however.

Height 46cm (18in)	**Weight** 11–12kg (24.25–16.5lb)
Exercise ***	**Grooming** *

Irish Water Spaniel

The Irish Water Spaniel is a striking looking animal with a mass of tightly curled liver coloured ringlets covering its body and a frizzy fringe over its forehead. Its origins are not clear. It was bred as a spaniel for water retrieving, but it bears an obvious resemblance to a Poodle.

They make a lovely pet suited to all ages.

Height 51–61cm (20–24in)	**Weight** 20.5–29.5kg (45–65lb)
Exercise ***	**Grooming** ***

Irish Wolfhound

The Wolfhound, as the name suggests, was initially bred for hunting wolves. It is a muscular, powerful dog with good stamina, yet gentle and docile as a pet.

The breed became rare in the 1800s after the wolf population became extinct in the UK but a breeding program started in the eighteenth century has restored the breed.

Irish Wolfhounds are excellent with children and other pets. They have a reliable, even temperament.

Height 81–86.5cm (32–34in)	**Weight** 47–55kg (103–121lb)
Exercise **	**Grooming** *

Italian Greyhound

The tiny graceful Italian Greyhound is a miniature version of the standard breed. While they are good athletes that do need plenty of exercise, these dogs like their indoor comforts and prefer to be kept as pets. They love nothing better than a soft, comfy sofa and the attentions of their owner.

This breed is suited to homes with older children, or adults.

Height 32–38cm (12.5–15in)	**Weight** 2.5–4.5kg (5.5–10lb)
Exercise **	**Grooming** *

Jack Russel Terrier

Jack Russel Terriers or 'Jacks' as they are affectionately known, are strong, muscular little 'pocket rockets'.

They are affectionate, exuberant and fearless. Jacks are also good 'ratters' and enthusiastic sheep and cattle dogs.

They make great companions, but need constant, patient training from an early age and should be supervised around young children and the elderly because the dog's darting movements can sometimes trip them!

Height 27–38cm (10.5–15in)	**Weight** 4–8kg (9–18lb)
Exercise ***	**Grooming** *

Japanese Chin

The Japanese Chin was introduced to Japan in the eight century B.C. It is a boisterous, merry and affectionate little dog that will play until it drops from exhaustion. The Chin is close to the perfect pet—it is intelligent, full of charm, gentle and clean. The smaller the size of a Japanese Chin, the better.

Height 30cm (12in)   **Weight** 2–3kg (4.5–6.5lb)
Exercise **   **Grooming*

Keeshond

The Keeshond is also called the Dutch Barge Dog. It was named after The rebel Dutch leader Cornelius (Kees) de Gyselaer and kept by his party as a symbol of resistance of the opposition.

They are a great watch dog and companion pet, but do require firm discipline and training.

The Keeshond is a playful, intelligent dog which loves children. They need their double coat brushed and de-matted regularly.

Height 43–46cm (17–18in)   **Weight** 13.6–20.4kg (30–45lb)
Exercise   **Grooming ***

Kerry Blue Terrier

The Kerry Blue Terrier stems from the farms of south western Ireland. It is thought to be a result of crosses between the Bedlington, Dandie Dinmont, and Irish Terriers and perhaps even the Irish Wolfhound.

This breed was used as a good all-rounder for many years in Ireland where it was a fighter, hunter, herder and even a butter churner. In 1922, it was presented at the Cruffs Show in Great Britain and introduced to the USA.

Kerrys love human company. They are affectionate and gentle with people. They can be testy with other dogs and while they are very trainable they are a stubborn breed.

Height 46–48cm (18–19in) **Weight** 15–17kg (33–37.5lb)
Exercise ** **Grooming** ***

King Charles Spaniel

This breed probably originated in China or Japan. They were well established in France before being introduced to Britain in the 1500s. Ladies of the court are said to have sought winter warmth by keeping these little animals hidden under their enormous skirts.

They achieved huge popularity under the reign of King Charles II, who, some said, was more interested in playing with his dogs than ruling over his country.

The King Charles is affectionate, intelligent and an excellent pet for both small children and adults.

Height 26–32cm (10.25–12.5in) **Weight** 3.5–6.5kg (7.75–14.5lb)
Exercise * **Grooming** *

Labrador Retriever

Labradors are loved and respected worldwide as police dogs, guide dogs for the blind and heroic war dogs.

These dogs are powerfully built and excellent swimmers. They were once a valued crew member on every Newfoundland fishing boat. They were trained to jump overboard when the boats neared the shore, gather the ends of fish laden nets in their mouths and swim to shore where other members of the crew would empty the nets.

Labradors are exceptionally patient, intelligent and gentle. They are excellent with children, easy to obedience train, and, not surprisingly, are prized pets worldwide.

Height 54–62cm (21–24.5in)	**Weight** 25–34kg (55–75lb)
Exercise ***	**Grooming** *

Lakeland Terrier

The Lakeland Terrier is an alert dog with acute hearing that makes it a good watch dog. They were originally bred for hunting and killing foxes. These dogs are a hardy breed, good with children and needing a moderate amount of exercise and occasional professional grooming.

Height 37cm (14.5in)	**Weight** 8kg (17.5lb)
Exercise ***	**Grooming** ***

Lhasa Apso

Lhasa Apsos were originally bred in Tibet where they were kept as good luck charms. They were never sold, and only the male were ever given away as pets. They are great, alert guard dogs with a loud bark.

Lhasas bond closely with their owners, and are prone to suffering from separation anxiety if they are not well socialized and trained. They make good apartment pets as long as they get sufficient outdoor time.

They are a kind, obedient breed, good with chidren.

Height 22–28cm (8.5–11in)	**Weight** 5.5–7kg (12–15.5lb)
Exercise **	**Grooming** ***

Maltese

The Maltese was a widespread breed throughout the Mediterranean from earliest times. They arrived in Britain somewhere around the 1500s, where they were popular ladies' pets.

They are renowned for their beauty, but are also intelligent, affectionate, strong and hardy little watch dogs that make lovely family pets.

Height 20–25cm (8–10in)	**Weight** 2–4kg (4.5–9lb)
Exercise **	**Grooming** ***

Manchester Terrier

The Manchester Terrier comes in both a standard and toy sized breed, originally bred as a cross between the Black and Tan Terrier (now extinct), the Whippet and probably the West Highland White Terrier.

They were originally bred as a ratter and rabbit hunter and were popular 'rat pitters' as well.

Manchester Terriers are a lovely companion dog, suitable for town and country living. They are good watch dogs and can be trained, with patience. Manchesters need to be protected from the cold and are not suitable as a pet for young or active children as the dog can be easily injured by them.

Standard:

Height 38–41cm (15–16in)	**Weight** 5–9kg (11–20)
Exercise **	**Grooming** *

Toy:

Height 25–30cm (10–12in)	**Weight** under 5kg (11lb)
Exercise **	**Grooming** *

Maremma Sheep Dog

The Maremma Sheep Dog is a strongly built herding dog, bred for guarding its flock against foe. They make great guard dogs and can also be excellent family pets, with a fondness for children. They are lively, active and intelligent, but not especially easy to train and need plenty of exercise.

Height 25 to 30cm (10–12in)	**Weight** under 5kg (11lb)
Exercise ****	**Grooming** **

Mastiff

Also called the Old English Mastiff, these large powerful dogs were bred as fighters, put up against bears, bulls, lions, tigers and the Romans even had them fighting gladiators.

They are an excellent guard dog but with good training and socialisation, also make nice pets.

They like children but should be supervised due to their size.

Height 69–76cm (10.25–30in)   **Weight** 72–90kg (159–198.5lb)
Exercise **   **Grooming** *

Mexican Hairless

This is an ancient breed which some Aztecs believed was the earthly representative of Xolotl (their alternative name) the god charged with escorting the dead to the next world. The non Aztecs of the time considered them a delicacy as a food source.

Legends also credit this little dog with magic healing powers. It was believed that when this little dog was held close, diseases such as asthma and rheumatism as well as malaria were 'drawn out'.

This dog is sensitive, quiet and intelligent. They are lovely little dogs with happy, family oriented personalities.

In every litter, there is usually at least one 'powder puff' puppy with luxurious hair.

Height 28–50cm (11–20in)   **Weight** (not specified)
Exercise **   **Grooming** **

Newfoundland

The Newfoundland is one of the few dogs that is native to North America. These gentle dogs have become a symbol of devotion and courage worldwide. They have a rich history of service to man—carrying lifelines to stricken vessels, rescuing drowning victims, saving children from harm and helping fisherman with their nets.

Newfies also make wonderful, docile and gentle pets. They are loyal and playful, adore children (who they were originally developed to play with and protect). They are loyal in the extreme.

Lord Byron once said of the Newfoundland that they have all the virtues of man without his vices.

Height 56–71cm (22–27.5in)	**Weight** 50–68kg (110–150lb)
Exercise ***	**Grooming** **

Norfolk Terrier

The Norfolk Terrier until fairly recently in history, was considered the ear dropped variety of its sister breed, the Norwich. These are feisty, sturdy little watch dogs, needing easy care and are a good, transportable size.

They are an ideal family companion, easy to train, are comfortable in any climate and happy in the city or country

Height 25cm (10in)	**Weight** 5–5.5kg (11–12.5lb)
Exercise **	**Grooming** *

Norwich Terrier

This lively, shaggy, short legged little dog is one of the smallest of the working terriers.

They were believed to be descendants of a small Irish terrier, the Cantab Terrier, which was then bred with other hard working terriers such as the Bedlington, and the Staffordshire Bull Terrier.

This plucky little breed make charming pets.

Height 25cm (10in)	**Weight** 5–5.5kg (11–12.5lb)
Exercise**	**Grooming***

Old English Sheepdog

The Old English Sheepdog was developed by sheep farmers in the English West Country, who used them mostly as drovers, driving livestock to market. Because working dogs were exempt from taxation, these dogs had their tails docked as proof of their occupation.

These dogs are boisterous, extremely affectionate and love to play with children. They are said to watch over children with the same degree of care they showed their flock, giving them the nickname of 'nanny dog' in the movie, *Peter Pan*.

They are an ideal family dog and also enjoy the company of other dogs in the household.

Height 56cm (22in)	**Weight** 27–45kg (59.5–99lb)
Exercise *	**Grooming ***

Papillon

The little Papillon is a charming vivacious dog and considered one of the most elegant breeds. It has been kept as a pet and source of amusement by royalty for centuries.

Papillons are excellent watch dogs, having a very keen sense of hearing. They can play for hours on end but can also be gentle, calm and patient. This breed can be possessive and jealous.

Height 20–28cm (8–11in)	**Weight** under 1.5kg (3.3lb)
Exercise **	**Grooming** **

Pekingese

Pekingese dogs are said to be miniature versions of the Foo Dog, an ancient Chinese animal that was said to ward off evil spirits. Pekingese were bred and reserved at the imperial palace in China for centuries. During the 1800s, at the height of their popularity, there were thousands of these dogs in Peking, and thousands of servants charged with their care.

In line with their pampered history, the modern day Peke is a gentle and affectionate but at times stubborn lap dog. They much prefer the couch to vigorous exercise. They are great with kids.

Height 15–23cm (6–9in)	**Weight** 2–8kg (4.5–17.5lb)
Exercise*	**Grooming** **

Pinscher

The Pinscher is sometimes mistaken for a miniature Doberman. It has existed in Germany for over 350 years, but its exact origins are unclear. Some sources believe it to be almost a shorthaired Schnauzer.

These dogs are easily trained, make good watch dogs and are well suited to indoor life as long as they get plenty of exercise.

Height 40–48cm (15.75–19in) **Weight** 12–16kg (26.5–35.5lb)
Exercise *** **Grooming** *

Pointer

Also known as the English Pointer, the Pointer is believed to have originated as a cross of both the French and Spanish Pointers. The job of a pointer is to point out the position of a hidden game, before flushing it.

The Pointer is a very intelligent, companionable breed. They need training and take a while to mature. They love humans and also get along well with other pets.

Height: 63–70cm (25–27.5in) **Weight** 18–25kg (40–55lb)
Exercise **** **Grooming** *

Pomeranian

The Pomeranian is the smallest member of the 'Spitz' breeds. They are an attractive, long haired breed with a luxurious tail and mane.

These dogs achieved great popularity in the late 1800s, when Queen Victoria took a great interest in them, and began selectively breeding them for small size, resulting in the modern day diminutive breed.

Poms have a natural gift for learning tricks and are great entertainers. They have been used as circus performers. They have a bark much larger than their bite, making good watch dogs and can be obedient and affectionate pets. They are clever, obedient, extroverted dogs that are easy to train and adore children.

Height 22–28cm (8.5–11in)	**Weight** 1.5–3.25kg (3.5–7lb)
Exercise **	**Grooming** ***

Poodle

The first poodles were large gun dogs with a special talent for retrieving birds from water. These dogs were of the standard breed, and were the forerunners of the other poodle types, being the miniature, toy and teacup. Poodles have a tightly curled woolen coat which needs clipping regularly. The traditional poodle clip was evolved largely out of practicality—the body was clipped short to allow for swimming, fur was left long on the legs and forequarters and over the kidneys to protect joints and vital organs from the cold.

Poodles are bright, amusing pets whose intelligence and trainability have gained them worldwide recognition. They love exercise and enjoy the company of children.

Toy:

Height: 25.5cm (10in) or under	**Weight** 2.5–5kg (5.5–11lb)
Exercise **	**Grooming** ****

Minature:

Height: 25.5–38cm (10–15in)	**Weight** 6.5–8kg (14.25–17.5lb)
Exercise ***	**Grooming** ****

Standard:

Height: 55–69 cm (21.5–27in)	**Weight** 20.5–32kg (45–70.5)
Exercise ****	**Grooming** *

Pug

Pugs are plucky little dogs with a distinctive squashed wrinkly, black face and tightly cured tail. This breed has been a source of amusement and company for many ancient royal s all over the world. They have been recorded in history in China, Britain, Holland, France and Spain.

Although they have been traditionally a companion to nobility and the wealthy, they are now common and popular family pets. These dogs are cleaver and mischievous. They can also be gluttonous, sulky and distant with strangers.

Height 30–35cm (12–13.75in)   **Weight** 6.25–8.25kg (13.75–18lb)
Exercise **   **Grooming** **

Puli

The Hungarian Puli is one of the most popular breeds in Hungary. It has a distinctive and glamorous shaggy, dense coat with a dreadlocked appearance.

Pulis are lively, agile dogs with a quick, bouncy gait. They are affectionate, loyal companions, if not a little stubborn.

Height 37–47cm (15–18.5in)   **Weight** 13–15kg (28.5–33lb)
Exercise **   **Grooming** **

Pyrenean Mountain Dog

The Pyrenean Mountain Dog was used to guard livestock in the chilly pastures of the Pyrenees. This is an alert and quick witted breed. They were used as sentries on French estates for many years.

Pyrenean Mountain Dogs make gentle, affectionate and obedient pets. They prefer to have plenty of outdoor time.

Height 64–81cm (25–32in)	**Weight** 41–57kg (90.5–125lb)
Exercise ***	**Grooming** ***

Rhodesian Ridgeback

The Rhodesian Ridgeback originates not from Zimbabwe as its name suggests, but from South Africa. It is, in fact, the only recognized breed to come from there. Ridgebacks were originally fearless hunters of lions and other big game-tracking, chasing and driving the animals towards the hunters.

They are good natured and trainable dogs that make good, if large, family pets.

Height 61–69cm (24–27in)	**Weight** 29.5–36.25cm (65–80lb)
Exercise ***	**Grooming** *

Rottweiler

Rottweliers are an imposing, muscular breed, supple athletes capable of reaching fast speeds. The Rottwelier makes a formidable guard dog. It is aloof with those other than its master, and while it's not suspicious of strangers, it will react swiftly when confronted with danger.

This breed is remarkably alert and intelligent, easy to obedience train, and a devoted pet.

Rotties are good, even tempered family pets that love and protect children.

Height 55–69cm (21.5–27in)	**Weight** 50kg (110lb)
Exercise ***	**Grooming** *

Saint Bernard

This noble breed has its origins in the Saint Bernard Hospice in Switzerland. Here it was bred by Monks for centuries and became famous for its legendary rescues in the Swiss Alps. The Saint Bernard's sense of smell enables him to scent a human against the wind up to two miles away, and sense blizzards and avalanches up to 20 minutes before they occur. His ability to locate bodies buried in as much as three metres of snow has resulted in him finding countless travellers trapped in drifts and leading them to safety.

Affectionately known as a Saint, the Saint Bernard is the genial gentleman of the canine world—very powerful but extremely placid. He adores children, and makes an intelligent, loyal and affectionate companion dog. His deep resonant bark is a marvellous deterrent to burglars. His hallmark is his huge, majestic head and benevolent dignified expression. He may be either rough or smooth coated.

Naturally a dog of this size requires room and is expensive to feed. But the rewards of owning one of these gentle giants more than compensates—just ask any Saint Bernard owner!

Height: 65–70cm (25.5–27.5in) **Weight** 55–60kg (121–132)

Exercise *** **Grooming *****

Saluki

The Saluki is a member of the Greyhound family. It is one of the oldest known breeds of dog that has remained almost unchanged for thousands of years. Those who appreciate beauty will fall in love with the elegant lines and graceful face of a Saluki. Legend has it that the Pharoah Antef enshrined his own pet in his tomb to have its spirit accompany him into the after life.

Salukis are quiet, one-person dogs. They are gentle and love to run.

Height 58–71cm (23–28in) **Weight** 14–25kg (31–55lb)

Exercise *** **Grooming ***

Samoyed

The Samoyed breed has been in the company of humans since it was first developed for herding reindeer and pulling sledges in Siberia.

As a result, these dogs have a special bond with humans. They are gentle and kind spirited and they adore the company of children. These dogs are intelligent and affectionate. They need plenty of exercise and grooming.

Height 46–56cm (18–22in) **Weight** 20–27kg (44–59.5lb)

Exercise *** **Grooming *****

Schipperke

The Schipperke has his origins on the riverboats and barges of Belgium where he was used both as a watch dog and for keeping vermin under control.

These dogs are a big personality in a little package. They are active little busy bodies and great watch dogs. The Schipperke is good with families.

Height 30cm (12in)	**Weight** 5.5–7.5kg (12–16.5lb)
Exercise ***	**Grooming** *

Schnauzer

The Miniature Schnauzer is the most popular of the three Schnauzer breeds, the other two being the Standard and the Giant.

This is the perfect small sized dog. They don't shed, are happy living inside and out, but do require regular exercise and should have their coat clipped intermittently.

Shnauzers are a very friendly, gentle breed, outstanding with children.

Height 33–35.5cm (13–14in)	**Weight** 7–10kg (15.5–22lb)
Exercise ***	**Grooming** **

Scottish Terrier

The 'Scottie' is the national dog of Scotland. These are an agile, independent breed, with a powerful build that belies their small size. Scottish terriers have a distinctly aristocratic look.

They tend to be a one-owner dog, are very wary of strangers and are a more suitable pet for adults than families with young children.

Height 25.4–28cm (10–11in) **Weight** 8.6–10.4kg (19–23lb)
Exercise **   **Grooming** **

Shetland Sheepdog

The Shetland Sheepdog, or 'Sheltie' as it is more commonly known, has its origins on the Shetland Islands, off Scotland's north coast. The harsh, cold climate of these islands along with the scarcity of food has resulted in a larger dog becoming a small one, much like many other animal breeds on the island.

Shelties are quiet, intelligent dogs. They make excellent little watch dogs are intensely loyal and affectionate with their owners and are excellent dogs to obedience train.

Height 37cm (15in) **Weight** approx 8kg (17.5lb)
Exercise **   **Grooming** ***

Shih-Tzu

The Shih Tzu is one of the few breeds that was developed not to do a job, but to luxuriate in the company of humans. The Shih Tzu is actually a descendant of the Lhasa Apso and Pekingese. These dogs were once considered sacred and a popular pet of the Chinese royal family throughout the Ming dynasty.

While Shihs are not ideal dogs for obedience training, they are great comedians who love to perform tricks, and they adore being the centre of attention. They are wary of strangers and make good watch dogs.

Height 23–26.7cm (9–11in)   **Weight** 4.5–8.1kg (10–18lb)
Exercise *   **Grooming** ***

Siberian Husky

Siberian Huskies were originally used as sled dogs by the Chukchi people of north eastern Asia. They were later used in the Antarctic expeditions and by the USA Army search and rescue unit during World War II.

Huskies are amazing athletes with outstanding stamina and endurance. This needs to be remembered if you are considering owning one as a pet. They need a great deal of exercise.

Huskies are affectionate, gentle dogs,. Although they are alert, they lack the protective instincts of other breeds so don't make great guard dogs. These dogs have a tendency to roam, so as well as needing plenty of exercise, they must be well fenced.

Height 51–60cm (20–23.5in)   **Weight** 20–27kg (44–59.5lb)
Exercise ****   **Grooming** **

Skye Terrier

This fearless, tough little cookie of a terrier, gets his name from the Isle of Skye, where he was kept as a vermin catcher. He has also been used for hunting and overtaking game.

Skye Terriers are unswervingly loyal and devoted to those they love, but are distrustful of strangers. They tend to be a one-person dog. This breed is intelligent and enjoys a lot of exercise. They are best suited to adult households or those with older children.

Height 23–26cm (9–10in)	**Weight** 8.6–11.3kg (19–25lb)
Exercise ***	**Grooming** **

Staffordshire Bull Terrier

This is a British breed which was developed by crossing the Bulldog with various local terriers. While Staffies were originally bred as fighting dogs, today they are one of the kindest and most friendly dogs around. These dogs are playful and loving. They adore children and adults and make excellent pets. Staffies have retained a tendency to be aggressive with other dogs, so are best suited to being the only dog in the household.

Height 36–41cm (14–16in)	**Weight** 12–17kg (26.5–37.5lb)
Exercise **	**Grooming** *

Tibetan Spaniel

The Tibetan Spaniel is an ancient breed of dog. It was originally developed by the Tibetan monks, who used them to turn the prayer wheels and as guard dogs.

Today they are the ideal lap dog. They love the company of their owners but dislike strangers.

Height 25–27cm (10–11in)	**Weight** 2–6kg (4.5–13.25lb)
Exercise *	**Grooming** **

Tibetan Terrier

Like the Tibetan Spaniel, the Tibetan Terrier is also believed to be bred by the Tibetan monks, and for many years were considered a symbol of good luck.

These dogs are lively, playful animals. They don't need a lot of exercise and are easy to train. Tibetan Terriers are good watch dogs with a bark much larger than their size. They are distrustful of strangers.

Height 35–40cm (13.75–15.75in) **Weight** 8–13.5kg (17.50–30lb)
Exercise *   **Grooming** **

Vizsla

Also called the Hungarian Vizsla, Vizslas are a hardworking, active field dog. They are more suited to very active families and better kept on acreage than in an urban environment.

They require a great deal of exercise to prevent them from becoming bored and unruly. Vizslas are intelligent and easy to train. Training is vital if they are to become controllable pets.

Height 53–64cm (21–25.25in) **Weight** 22–30kg (48.5–66lb)
Exercise ****   **Grooming** *

Weimaraner

The Weimeraner originated in Germany where it was first used for hunting large game, and then as a water retriever.

These dogs make excellent, intelligent pets and is one of the best behaved breeds, as long as it is obedience trained ad gets plenty of exercise. They love children.

Height 56–70cm (22–27.5in) **Weight** 32–39kg (70.5–86lb)
Exercise ****   **Grooming** *

Welsh Corgi

There are two types of Welsh Corgis, the Cardigan and the Pembroke. Both breeds make tough, fearless little working dogs that are actually quick runners despite their short legs.

Corgis are very protective of their owner and possessions and, especially the Cardigan, is very suspicious of strangers, making them excellent guard dogs.

Corgis are lovely pets. They are gentle, intelligent, loyal and affectionate, especially with children.

Height 25–30cm (10-12in)	**Weight** 8–11kg (17.5–24.25lb)
Exercise ***	**Grooming** **

Welsh Springer Spaniel

A well trained Welsh Springer Spaniel is arguably the best gun dog there is. This breed is extremely intelligent and easy to obedience train. Yet they also make an excellent house dog. As long as they get plenty of exercise, they are quite happy in an urban environment. They get along very well with children and other animals.

Height 46–48cm (18–19in)	**Weight** 16–20.5kg (35.25–45.25lb)
Exercise ***	**Grooming** **

Welsh Terrier

The Welsh Terrier actually originated in England, but it was the Welsh who developed it into a sporting dog, breeding it to hunt badgers, fox and otters.

Welsh Terriers need good obedience training and early socialisation with other dogs if they are to be reliable with them.

They are an energetic, warm and affectionate breed, especially suited to a lively, active family.

Height 38cm (15in)   **Weight** 9kg (20lb)
Exercise ***   **Grooming** *

West Highland White Terrier

The Westie shares its lineage with the 'Scottie', the Cairn and the Dandie-Dinmont terrier, all of which were bred to keep foxes, otters and other vermin under control on farms in Scotland.

They are spirited and courageous little dogs. They will settle nicely into a family with children, but are even better without. They have a lovely pure white coat, but the trade off for this is that they shed fur.

Height 28cm (11in)   **Weight** 7–10kg (15.5–22lb)
Exercise **   **Grooming** ***

Whippet

The whippet is an elegant dog that looks a little like a miniature English Greyhound.

This is the fastest domestic dog for its size, able to reach speeds of up to 55km per hour within seconds. Whippets do not shed and keep themselves very clean. They love children and are quite happy to live in an apartment, as long as they get a good run each day.

Whippets like to make a 'nest' for themselves when they sleep—so it is wise to give them their own blanket to avoid a house full of unmade beds.

Height 44–56cm (17.5–22in)   **Weight:** not specified
Exercise ***   **Grooming** *

Yorkshire Terrier

Yorkies are one of the most glamorous and popular of all the toy breeds of dog. These days, they are often seen in handbags, pimped and pruned to be shown off. It's hard to believe the breed was originally used to control the rat population in the Yorkshire mines and cotton mills.

Over the years, the breed have been selectively bred to become smaller and smaller, but they have little dynamite personalities, reminiscent of the larger dog they used to be.

They are loveable, intelligent and affectionate. Because they are small, they make ideal apartment dogs.

Height under 20cm (8in)   **Weight** up–3.5kg (7.75lb)
Exercise *   **Grooming** ***

Crossbreed dogs

The 'oodles'

Poodle cross breed dogs have become very popular in recent times. Part of the appeal of a poodle cross is the possibility of a non-shedding, odourless coat, and the plucky, active temperament of the poodle combined with the temperament and physical traits of the breed it is crossed with.

Some Examples are:

- Labrador cross Poodle—'Labradoodle'
- Spaniel cross Poodle—'Spoodle'
- Cavalier King Charles Spaniel cross Poodle—'Cavoodle'
- Schnauzer cross poodle—'Schnoodle'

At the time of writing this book, the crosses were not registered as pure breeds of dog.

It should be noted that a non-shedding coat cannot be guaranteed, and temperament not necessarily predicted.

Because of the combination of breeds, these dogs are less likely to be affected by hereditary genetic problems.

Further Reading

Behaviour Problems in Dogs and Cats, Henry. R. Asken

Flea Control and Surgery Aftercare information taken from Mosman Vet Hospital client handout.

Good information on breed types, bite statistics and taining tips can be found on the Pet Care Information and Advisory Centre website.

www.petnet.com.au
www.urbananimal.net
www.aspca.org
www.rspca.org.uk
www.rspca.org.au
www.mosmanvetclinic.com.au

About the author

Rachele Lowe is a practising veterinarian, TV presenter and weekly columnist in national magazines.

After regular segments on the *Lifestyle Channel*, Rachele has been the resident vet on *Sunrise* and the *Morning Show* since 2003, with the assistance of her lovable, well-trained dog Minou.

Rachele is co-owner of the successful Mosman Veterinary Hospital in Sydney, and has plenty of on-the-job experience in animal care, maintenance and behaviour. The Mosman Veterinary Hospital provides services in small animal medicine and surgery, dentistry, diagnostic imaging, pathology and preventative care.

First published in Australia in 2009 by
New Holland Publishers (Australia) Pty Ltd
Sydney • Auckland • London • Cape Town

1/66 Gibbes Street Chatswood NSW 2067 Australia
218 Lake Road Northcote Auckland New Zealand
86 Edgware Road London W2 2EA United Kingdom
80 McKenzie Street Cape Town 8001 South Africa

A record of this book is held at the National Library of Australia

ISBN 9781741108125

Publishers: Linda Williams and Fiona Schultz
Publishing Manager: Lliane Clarke
Editors: Christine Chua and Ashlea Wallington
Designer: Tania Gomes
Production Manager: Olga Dementiev
Printer: McPhersons Printing Group, Maryborough

10 9 8 7 6 5 4 3 2 1